In *Business by Design,* Raymond Harris invites us to see the real-world brilliance of Jesus as it applies to the practical strategy, decision-making, people management, and deeper purpose of business and enterprise. For leaders seeking first-class excellence in both entrepreneurial endeavors and Christian integrity of life, Harris delivers a thoughtful meditation and testimony on what it looks like to apply the profound spiritual teachings of Jesus to the pragmatic, real-life challenges of business endeavors at the highest level.

—GARY HAUGEN, *founder and CEO of International Justice Mission*

Business by Design is a game changer, but not because it teaches a new business theory. Rather, it is built on the timeless truths of the Bible. It is wonderfully authentic because the author, Raymond Harris, has lived the principles he is communicating. I heartily recommend it!

—HOWARD DAYTON, *founder and CEO of Compass*

Business by Design captures the essence of doing business by God's design. Whether working, running a business, or serving in a ministry, Raymond articulates these business principles and shares his personal stories that apply to today's world. I recommend this to every working professional.

—JOSH MCDOWELL, *speaker and author*

Raymond Harris is a unique visionary who has found his most remarkable of professional opportunities with the church and its mission at the intersection of life and business, where he shares Christ as he does in the pages of *Business by Design.*

—KEITH & KRISTYN GETTY, *modern hymn writers,*
Music

My big-hearted friend Ray[ ] God
trusted with little. Raymond[ ] mond
with much, and he remai[ ] strates

that principle so well and is instructive to those who need to learn to be trusted with little, so that God might trust them with much!

—Bob Doll, *chief equity strategist for Nuveen Asset Management*

For anyone seeking true success in life and business, this book is bursting with biblical wisdom and practical advice! Read this book and learn from Raymond's experience of operating businesses as a way to love people and build God's kingdom.

—Todd Harper, *president of Generous Giving*

Raymond Harris has written a warm and inviting reflection on his forty-year faith journey in the marketplace. This is a fantastic read!

—Dr. Mac Pier, *author, founder and CEO of Movement.org*

Brimming with countercultural and actionable insights, *Business by Design* is a powerful and engaging read. This book is highly readable and relevant for every type of business or nonprofit context. You will love this book!

—Peter Greer, *president and CEO of HOPE International and coauthor of* Rooting for Rivals

Saturated in the Scriptures and filled with practical wisdom, *Business by Design* is a work of love that will bless your circle of influence. Raymond's keen insights and personal stories will appeal to both the head and the heart. If you are looking for next steps in how you might be a light in your world, look no further.

—Adam C. Wright, PhD, *president of Dallas Baptist University*

Business by Design builds on Raymond Harris' lifetime of experience of building an architectural firm that's successful by any definition, and he lays out practical, biblical principles that anyone who wants to have a life that counts can depend on.

—Kevin Palau, *author, president and CEO of Luis Palau Association*

Business by Design is a useful tool that provides a guide to the reader on how to balance the cut-throat world of business practices with one's faith. This is a difficult road to travel, but Raymond gives us a roadmap. It is up to us to determine whether we choose to follow it.

—MIKE MONCREIF, *former mayor of Fort Worth, Texas*

In *Business by Design*, Raymond Harris masterfully explores the teachings of Jesus of Nazareth, anchors business practices to core biblical principles, and reveals the purpose of business in a kingdom economy. This is a must-read for business leaders, young professionals, nonprofit executives, ministry leaders, and pastors.

—ALBERT L. REYES, PhD, *president and CEO of Buckner International*

Business by Design brings to life the teachings of Jesus as a practical guide to building businesses that expand His kingdom on earth. Using real-life stories from his own successful architectural firm, Raymond Harris reminds us that in God's hands, business is one of the most powerful instruments of economic, social, and spiritual transformation. It's a great read for faith-centered business leaders seeking to live a life of meaning.

—J. DALE DAWSON, *former investment banker, entrepreneur, founder and CEO of Bridge to Rwanda*

In a simple but profound manner, this book captures the very essence of leadership. Harris understands that success doesn't come from accumulating, emphasizing our accomplishments, or making a name for ourselves. Success comes from prayerfully and thoughtfully giving away our talents, our treasures, and our time—that's true success in God's economy.

—STEVE SHACKELFORD, *CEO of Redeemer City to City*

You can't spend five minutes with Raymond and not gain amazing nuggets of wisdom of God's heart towards money. I've learned so much about stewardship and transferring wealth to heavenly treasures. You are in for a treat as you read *Business by Design*. Having walked with him over the years on multiple endeavors, I can attest that he practices what he is teaching here.

—ANDREW ERWIN, *president of Erwin Brothers Entertainment*

If you have a love for business or are considering going into business but have a concern about how to set it up within the values and standards of God, so that you fulfill your mission as a business leader and do not find yourself getting choked out by the cares of the world, wealth, and pride of life, this is a book you should read.

—MORGAN JACKSON, *senior vice president of Faith Comes By Hearing*

I know of no other book that more powerfully and practically prepares business leaders to be successful in their earthly pursuits while becoming agents of transformation in their culture. I pray God will use this resource to change the future of business and mightily advance the kingdom of Christ.

—BYRON PAULUS, *president and CEO of Life Action Ministries*

This is a tremendously warm and practical book filled with encouraging, achievable examples from every area of business life. As I read it, I couldn't stop thinking of friends, relatives, and others in the business and professional world to whom I would recommend it. More than that, this is a book rooted in the Bible and prayer, and it is built on a strong Christian foundation.

—RAM GIDOOMAL, *commander of the most excellent order of the British Empire, former chairman of the Lausanne Movement International Board, chairman of South Asian Concern*

Christians need to understand how to apply their faith in the business arena because they live in the tension that exists between the world's economy and God's economy. This book shares both personal stories and key biblical principles that will help you integrate your faith with your work. Learn from a man who is a practicing architect, executive movie producer, and venture capitalist in God's kingdom.

—KERBY ANDERSON, *president of Probe Ministries,
host of radio talk show* Point of View

More than any other book, *Business by Design* is a practical, "how-to" manual from someone who wants to see those coming after him go beyond him, which to me is the mark of godly, servant leadership. Raymond Harris is a business leader whose entire life is ministry. I think we need more voices like that, and I pray this book can equip you to be one.

—NICK HALL, *founder of PULSE*

Behind every great design, there is purpose, function, and beauty. This book practically shows us how our hearts and minds can be rewired. Every reader will benefit from the wonderful stories of success and failure from a master architect who reveals the purpose of our Designer in our everyday lives.

—JACK ALEXANDER, *chairman of the Reimagine Group and
onQ, author of* The God Impulse *and* The God Guarantee

God's ways are higher than ours, but Raymond's use of God's Word will bless you and benefit your business. In *Business by Design*, Raymond Harris makes timeless biblical principles come alive in today's hypercompetitive business world. Raymond's personal stories give you concrete, next steps to make His kingdom come in your workplace. He doesn't forsake excellence in the pursuit of faithfulness, and you shouldn't hesitate to read this phenomenal work.

—NICK PITTS, PhD, *blogger, executive director
of the Institute for Global Engagement*

Every young man and woman entering the business world should read *Business by Design*! You will discover your work really does matter in God's economy. Prepare to be motivated and gain insight on how to bring your best every day!

—REED LIVESAY, *CEO of Pine Cove Camps*

Raymond has an excellent understanding of doing business using God's principles as boundaries and guidelines. It is rare to find a book written by a successful businessperson who is capable of giving business advice as well as direction on godly living. I wish he had written this for me many years ago, so I could have read it instead of the many books espousing principles that lead me down wrong paths.

—PHIL SMITH, *former CEO and chairman of Sermon.net, coauthor of* The Poor Will Be Glad *and* A Billion Bootstraps

Raymond Harris gives us biblical principles lived out in real-life circumstances. This book is helpful reading for the young business leader and those who hope to become business leaders.

—D.G. ELMORE, *chairman of Elmore Companies and The Navigators*

Raymond Harris has created a step-by-step guide on how to become a true steward in God's kingdom. He distinguishes between the world's economy and God's economy and how to be kingdom-minded in your approach to business.

—DARYL JOHNSTON, *television commentator, former football player for the NFL's Dallas Cowboys*

The revelation and insight that Raymond Harris has unearthed through the parables in the gospel are keys to true success. I would highly recommend *Business by Design* to everyone and anyone who is serious about unlocking the doors to wisdom, integrity, and fulfillment.

—REV. ADAM DURSO, DD, *executive director of LEAD.NYC*

Many books on business are written by leaders who have been mildly successful in their work, but Raymond Harris has been wildly successful, and he'd be the first to tell you it's been God all the way. The humble, honest, raw perspective shared in these pages are rich with Scripture and full of practical insight for anyone looking to lead a biblical life in a difficult world. Raymond has been integral to my growth as a leader, and I'm confident he'll be the same for you.

—GRANT SKELDON, *founder of Initiative Network*

For twenty years I've watched Raymond Harris design buildings and create goodwill with uncommon and godly decision-making. *Business By Design* is all about serving Jesus in the real world—with story after surprising story! Young business leaders will love reading *Business by Design* and asking themselves, "What would I do if I was in Raymond's shoes?"

—DAVE RINER, *executive director of Student Mobilization*

In *Business by Design*, Raymond takes the reader on a journey of discovery that's rooted deeply in the Scriptures. It quickly becomes clear that business and discipleship are joyfully and seamlessly interwoven. The personal nature of the stories in this book, the vulnerability of the writer, and the practical lessons all make this reading an enjoyable, soul-searching, and helpful experience.

—MUTUA MAHIAINI, *international president of The Navigators*

Business by Design is a tool for mentoring emerging, young, Christian professionals toward true success. Raymond Harris lays out the best practices for integrating faith with business, so that one can live a life of purpose and develop a heart of righteous character that leads to righteous actions toward the less fortunate and the marginalized. This is a must-read for anyone seeking to live a life of meaning with eternal dividends.

—CÉLESTIN MUSEKURA, *PhD, president and CEO of African Leadership and Reconciliation Ministries, Inc. (ALARM)*

As someone committed to preparing this next generation of leaders, I recommend this book to you. *Business by Design* is a compelling, visionary, and practical example of what it looks like to make a difference in this world for Jesus. You will be challenged to live for His glory as you live out your faith in the marketplace.

—MARK GAUTHIER, *vice president of Cru,*
executive director of Cru's US Campus Ministry

Business by Design is a tremendous resource for young business professionals who may be unsure of how their budding careers intersect with kingdom work. Harris' book is filled with both practical and inspiring biblical principles to help them succeed in finding that intersection. What's more, these principles prevail cultural boundaries and can be applied globally in any context. I highly recommend this book to those wanting to make their professional careers have a lasting and eternal impact on the world!

—DOUG SHAW, *president and CEO*
of International Students, Inc.

Business by Design is a practical, thoughtful understanding of God's work for the businessperson wanting to steward their career or company in a God-honoring manner. Raymond Harris provides personal examples, biblical insights, and encouraging models for the reader who desires to glorify God in their workplace. I encourage you to not only read the book, but also the take time to reflect upon the treasure of principles found within these pages!

—TRAE VACEK, *national director*
of Bridges International

I felt like I was sitting at the feet of a mentor because Raymond Harris reveals how he extends God's love to others through the day-to-day realities of engaging in business. If you care at all about influencing your organization's culture, you must read *Business by Design.*

—BILL HENDRICKS, *executive director for Christian Leadership,*
The Hendricks Center at Dallas Theological Seminary, coauthor of
Your Work Matters to God, *author of* The Person Called YOU:
Why You're Here, Why You Matter & What You
Should Do With Your Life

BUSINESS BY DESIGN

Applying God's Wisdom for True Success

RAYMOND HARRIS

BroadStreet
PUBLISHING

BroadStreet Publishing® Group, LLC

Savage, Minnesota, USA

BroadStreetPublishing.com

BUSINESS BY DESIGN: *Applying God's Wisdom for True Success*

Stock or custom editions of BroadStreet Publishing titles may be purchased in bulk for educational, business, ministry, fundraising, or sales promotional use. For information, please email info@broadstreetpublishing.com.

Dan Balow, literary agent at The Steve Laube Agency

Cover design by Chris Garborg at garborgdesign.com

Interior design and typesetting by Katherine Lloyd at theDESKonline.com

Printed in the United States of America

18 19 20 21 22 5 4 3 2 1

CONTENTS

FOREWORD

Our business partnership with Raymond over the past twenty years is a remarkable story. We can attest to the genuine, purposeful commitment Raymond made as a young man to live and work by faith. For Raymond, there is no distinction between faith and business: his business is the evidence of his faith.

Raymond's insightful study of the Gospels shines a light on business principles woven into the teachings of Jesus and gleaned from his interpersonal relationships. The anecdotal stories from Raymond's personal journey provide relatable accounts for all who desire to live out their faith in the workplace.

Just as we have been blessed in our relationship with Raymond, we pray that you will be blessed by the simple truths he shares in the following chapters.

—Shade O'Quinn and Larry Craighead
Partners in Raymond Harris & Associates Architects,
one of the most prolific large architectural firms in the US

PREFACE

I am an architect.

I've been trained to design buildings and to build things. It is safe to say that everyone I've met in America has been in a building that my firm has either designed or remodeled. Not many architects can boast such a claim, but I realize it is a result of God's faithful blessing upon us. In reality, I know our success is a gift.

I enjoy leading people to build our company—now one of the most prolific architectural firms in the country and serving some of the world's largest clients. And I realize this would have been impossible without seeking God's wisdom through the application of his business principles found in the Gospel parables. In this book I have attempted to share what I have learned over the past thirty-five years.

In order to apply these biblical business principles, I had to reprogram my heart and rewire my thinking about how I approach business and the people I lead. I hope this book may help you reprogram your thinking as you work or build your business.

Since the master Architect has clearly laid out a plan for us to follow, my goal is to demonstrate faithful obedience in what I understand that design to be.

Over thirty-five years ago, I had breakfast with J. Oswald Sanders, a well-known Christian author. Mr. Sanders, a lawyer and ministry leader, was well up in years and respected for the wisdom he shared through his published writings. I asked him to write a book for young professionals that would show us how to be effective in the workplace. Without hesitation, he said, "Why don't you write that book? You are the one who seems to need it."

That statement has haunted me and now convicted me to write this very book.

1

PURPOSE, PROFIT, AND SUCCESS

I was usually comfortable on the open road behind the wheel of my 1983 Honda Accord—especially with Marydel sitting next to me. But on one particular day, not so much. I suppose some of it was fear of being late for the most important meeting I had ever had in my young architectural business. Some of it was probably the gnawing sense in my stomach that I didn't belong in this meeting—who was I to deserve an audience with one of the nation's largest retail companies?

I kept trying to talk myself out of the recurring nightmare that played in my mind: wise, experienced businessmen on the other side of an enormous table who were unable to stop laughing at the audacity of a twenty-eight-year-old architect with a skinny portfolio taking up their valuable time. As if I could deliver something they needed. The nightmare, of course, played into my fears of unworthiness and inexperience. Marydel, bless her heart, was my biggest cheerleader and helped me drive on with determination.

The stoplight-studded old highway to Bentonville, Arkansas, from our Fayetteville hotel offered all kinds of opportunities to delay us on that cool, rainy morning. Even though I was excitedly nervous, I definitely did not want the tense driving conditions to make us late. Pressing hard on the wheel, I prayed that we would make it on time. The bright side of me was ecstatic about the rare prospect of meeting with the powerhouses behind this company's meteoric rise to retail dominance. I kept trying to reassure myself: *At least I won't walk away from this meeting with less than I had when I walked in.*

I also kept telling myself that this was not exactly an awkward cold call. In fact, this potential client had invited me to come based on a small project I had done indirectly for them just a year earlier. I had just left my employer—on good terms—to start my own business. A contractor offered them a small job that they deemed unworthy of their time and reputation. "We don't do this kind of work," they said. "But we can recommend a hungry young architect who would be glad to work with you on it."

When the contractor called, I said, "Absolutely!"

At that point, I didn't have the experience to back up my hope, but somehow I believed that small didn't always mean insignificant. I believed that if I gave it my best, it might open the door to something greater. I had heard of the principle, "Whoever can be trusted with very little can also be trusted with much" (Luke 16:10 NIV). This Scripture was instrumental in helping me start and build a company that would one day serve wonderful clients.

It just so happened that this contractor's small project was for a client named Walmart, the retail giant. And at some point, they had taken notice of the project and my part in it and decided that I might be open to doing more work for them.

Marydel and I finally arrived at our destination. My nightmare immediately vanished as I saw the humble warehouse. I parked the car in the gravel parking lot and walked through unassuming storefront doors into a small waiting area with inexpensive folding chairs. After a few minutes, a gracious Mike Webb sat down with me to discuss possible work for our firm.

What an exhilarating surprise it was. I had thought I was coming to introduce myself with the possible hope of a future project that could blossom into more. Instead, I left the building with nineteen small projects waiting for me to start. Thank God I hadn't let fear talk me into a U-turn.

The Tension between Two Economies

Can you see the two realms and their conflicting economies? The world's economy operates only in the physical world into which you were born; you naturally believe it to be the most real. God's economy operates in the spiritual world that is unseen by your eyes; it calls you into a greater and more enduring reality— a reality that the physical can never provide.

Following God's direction wholeheartedly means choosing his world, his economy, his kingdom over the pull of this fallen world and its values. It means taking a long-term view that doesn't get sucked in by shortcuts. It means believing that if you put God first and value others as you value yourself, then you will come out ahead; not ahead of others necessarily, because this is not a competition, but ahead of where you can ever get by putting yourself first.

Which economy will you give priority to? Which one defines your identity and gives you purpose?

Although you presently live in both economies, only one can take priority. No matter which one you choose to put first, the choice relies on faith, because no one can prove God's existence or nonexistence. And regardless of which economy you put first, you will always feel the tension between the two. Your choice has to be continually reaffirmed and proven through your actions. Furthermore, your choice continues to define your identity and your purpose in an ongoing way. Which economy do you choose to serve? Which identity and purpose will drive your personal and business development?

I hope you'll stick with me through this journey, because it's not easy to unseat the assumptions that form your perspective on this choice. Look carefully at the success characteristics I introduce as opposed to the world's approach that appears to work but then either blows up or leads to unquenchable thirst.

Purposes for Business

There are numerous purposes for business presented in the parables and teachings of Jesus. But the emphasis on certain principles suggests primary purposes for building a business to further God's kingdom on earth. The primary purposes I have gleaned are:

- To love and honor God.
- To love others and do what is best for them.
- To seek God's kingdom and his righteousness.
- To develop and transfer treasures to heaven.

These purposes are accomplished by bearing the fruit of righteousness. Jesus said that the kingdom of heaven is given to those who are producing its fruit. How do we know if we are accomplishing these purposes and bearing fruit that lasts for eternity? We need to understand our broader purpose on earth so that we may determine our particular purpose in work and business.

What Is My Purpose on Earth?

Many of us wonder, but few of us take the time to think deeply through our purpose on earth. Two basic questions come to mind when I think about my purpose on earth:

1. Who am I to become?
2. What am I to do?

From my study of Jesus' parables, the answers seem to be that I am to be a person of righteous character who is rich in good deeds, and I am to do the work of Christ on this earth by being his hands and feet.

When God saves our souls, he transforms our purpose from glorifying ourselves to glorifying him. As such, we are to be good workers who are unashamed of the gospel as we build up the body of Christ. We are to be fierce soldiers who fight injustice and protect the weak. Finally, we are to work out our salvation with a healthy fear of God that is expressed through our righteous actions; we are to work hard, knowing that we will one day stand before the Lord to give an account of our lives. This healthy fear of God is really a respect and love for him as our Creator and Master.

Loving and Honoring God

As I have contemplated why God gave me the ability to establish and maintain a large architectural firm, I have become convinced that it was to glorify him by being a faithful steward of my business opportunities while serving those around me. Part of my stewardship is to generate profit in my business, just like the faithful stewards in the parables. But I am also to pursue constant fellowship with God and intimately abide in him so that the fruit born through me will show my love and devotion to him.

Loving Others While Working

While studying the Gospels, I was constantly reminded of the importance of loving others through the application of the Golden Rule in all things business. Knowing that the souls of people last for eternity, I consider it an imperative to love people in such a way that they see the kingdom of God in all that I do. In addition to telling them about God's love, showing love through my actions is the most effective witness. There is no greater way to express love in the daily work environment than by doing what is in the best interest of employees, clients, and all business associates.

There is no division between the sacred and secular when it comes to working in business. Everything we do at work should be done to the glory of God. All business is important, and everything should be done to advance the kingdom of God. There is nothing more holy than performing excellent work while employing people and sharing the gospel through how you run a business. We positively affect a lot of people when we handle our business in accordance with God's principles.

In a construction shack years ago, a job superintendent said something that floored me. "I notice something different about you," he said. "You haven't said it, but the way you act makes me wonder if you're a Christian."

"Yes, I am," I answered.

"I knew because of the way you treat me and others on this job," he told me. "I also notice it in how you handle problems."

That conversation has stuck with me for over twenty years.

Throughout the years, several other building contractors have told me that they sensed there was something different in how I handle business. It was affirming to know that as I sought to show love to others, I was expressing my deep faith in God. As an interesting side note, the relationship between a contractor and an architect is notoriously tense and filled with opportunities to blame each other. I have always taken the position that the contractor is an ally, and we must work effectively together to take good care of the client. With this attitude in mind, I have always developed a friendship with our contractors.

I do not want to wear my faith on my sleeve by only talking about it rather than showing it through my actions. Obviously, actions speak louder than words, and we should never be ashamed of our faith in Jesus. Humbly demonstrating our faith through our righteous actions is an effective way to share the love of God.

The Use of Profit

In my opinion, there are several priorities for the use of profit. First, we should take care of our immediate family. Second, we have an obligation to take care of our employee family, ensuring that employees can support their families and benefit by sharing in the company's profits. A generous work environment supports financially healthy employees who help sustain the business.

Profit should also be used to build and expand an economic engine so the company can remain vibrant and sustainable. If all profit is spent on excessive overhead and compensation, then nothing is available to fuel and maintain the engine generating those profits. Appropriate and prudent reinvestment in a company is critical for the healthy continuance of the economic business engine.

Once profits have been allocated to these three uses, where else should they be deployed? Should business owners use the remaining profit for their own exclusive consumption? Is there a greater purpose? As stewards in God's kingdom, business owners know that the entirety of their profits are not for personal consumption or hoarding. This is graphically depicted by the foolish rich farmer in Luke 12:18–21 (NIV):

> Then [the farmer] said, "This is what I'll do. I will tear
> down my barns and build bigger ones, and there I will
> store my surplus grain. And I'll say to myself, 'You have
> plenty of grain laid up for many years. Take life easy;
> eat, drink and be merry.'"
>
> But God said to him, "You fool! This very night your
> life will be demanded from you. Then who will get what
> you have prepared for yourself?"
>
> This is how it will be with whoever stores up things
> for themselves but is not rich toward God.

I think there is a higher purpose for our profits.

Deploying Profits for the Future

The disciple Timothy was to give instruction to the wealthy on how to deploy earthly profits and lay up treasure in heaven (1 Timothy 6:17–19). We are exhorted to be rich in good deeds and to be generous, willing to share with others. But we destroy the ability to share with others if we are totally geared toward consumption. Our earthly treasures are never to be hoarded but are to be distributed humbly. We are not to set our hopes on the uncertainty of riches, but set our hope on God, who richly provides us with everything for our enjoyment. Always be on the alert for deployment opportunities, ready for action, and quick to respond.

When I ask my friends what they want to hear when they stand before the Lord, I always hear the same thing. They want to hear, "Well done, good and faithful servant." That assumes they were servants of God and faithful stewards of what had been entrusted to them.

Everyone wants affirmation and to hear the words "well done." But to hear these words, we must heed Jesus' instructions in the Gospels on how to be good stewards. He told the rich young ruler, "Go, sell all that you have and give to the poor, and you will have treasure in heaven" (Mark 10:21). This promise from God assures that if we take care of the poor, then we will store up treasures in heaven. Taking care of the poor and the vulnerable is mentioned many times in Psalms and Proverbs. For example, Proverbs 19:17 tells us that we are actually loaning to God when we give to the poor and that he will repay us.

My Pledge to You

My life in business, with its rewarding successes and painful failures, has taught me a lot over the years. But my growing knowledge of God's Word has taught me even more. I could easily lay out a formula for success and promise you that following it would give you everything you ever wanted. But it would be neither honest nor true. It's not quite that simple—in part because we live in two economies.

It is my desire that this book be practical rather than philosophical. The biblical principles described in this book are extremely practical. They will help you in your pursuit of success in earthly business. I really believe that. But I don't guarantee success, because I have no idea how you define success. And I don't know God's path for you in his plan for your success.

Here's the best promise I can make to unlock business success: If you wholeheartedly follow God's direction, he *may* refine your concept of success, and he *will* give you the desires of your heart. If instead, you trust your eyes and the convincing deceptions of this temporary world, no success will *ever* satisfy your deepest longings.

2

BUSINESS IN GOD'S ECONOMY

The principles of business in God's economy are upside down from those of this world.

Suppose you decided to loan a promising young company a substantial amount of money to create something that would be a positive influence in the world. And suppose you followed good business principles and put your agreement in writing—a contract that specified all the repayment terms. And when the payment was finally due, the company was unable to pay. What do you do? You didn't see this coming, but now you have to deal with it.

That's exactly where I was at a few years ago. What I did about it is still being played out in ways I wouldn't have guessed. I'll tell you the whole story later because it is a prime example of our opening statement: The principles of business in God's economy are upside down from those of this world.

Unfortunately, even those of us who choose to serve God's

economy often fail to see through the world's deceptions. We rationalize what seems to work, justifying our lack of faith in God's principles by concluding that they must have been meant for a time in the past—or perhaps for a time in the future. But they are for *all* times, because, as we shall see, they are all based on love, which is an essential part of God's unchanging character. For us to comprehend God's economics, we must reprogram our brains and rewire our hearts to be kingdom-minded and eternity-driven business leaders.

Reprogram Our Brains and Rewire Our Hearts

How do we reprogram our brains and rewire our hearts? Well, God's direction for us—including how we conduct business—comes from his Word. Only the truth of his Word has the power to reprogram our brains and rewire our hearts. A casual awareness of what he says is insufficient; we need to act upon it. This often stretches our faith because it seems upside down from what we see all around us.

I made a promise to you in the first chapter: If you wholeheartedly follow God's direction, then he will develop and refine your concept of success and give you the desires of your heart, both now and forever. What do I mean by "God's direction"?

God's direction is the way he specifically speaks to you based on how you have prepared your heart and mind to hear and apply what he says. In my journey to reprogram and rewire, I have noticed layers in God's direction, thus enabling me to grow in my understanding and follow-through. Much of this book describes these various layers and the ways I have organized them to make his direction more productive in my life and business.

The Funnel

As a quick overview, picture these layers like a funnel that processes thoughts into actions. It might help to view them in a funnel like this:

Think of biblical principles as summary statements of how God has designed life to work in this world. Jesus taught and lived by them—even as the Pharisees accused him of breaking God's law. Jesus was living the spirit of the law while they were stumbling over their own perversion of it. He demonstrated how the funnel concept works.

Virtually every biblical principle (top of the funnel) can be applied as a business concept. To be real and more than just ideas, these principles and concepts must manifest in action. What we do speaks louder than words; we all despise the hypocrisy of those who don't walk their talk. God didn't just say "I love you;" he demonstrated it at the greatest possible cost to himself.

Like God, we demonstrate the reality of our principles through our actions. When you live out a biblical principle through a business concept, you do it through actions. These actions reflect God's righteous character, which is something far greater than mere platitudes. God's character blends truth and grace, holding them in perfect tension. For example, God is morally demanding, *and* he is merciful. He is holy, *and* he loves

15

us in our fallen, unholy condition. He demands perfection, *and* he supplies it because we are incapable of it.

But there is another vital aspect of actions too: they not only demonstrate reality, but they also create it. You become a certain kind of person by doing what that kind of person does. You become a compassionate person, for example, by choosing to act for the benefit of someone else—one person at a time, one situation at a time. Little by little it becomes a habit, and little by little you become known as a compassionate person.

Back to the layers of God's direction: we'll deal with them from the top of the funnel down, just as our brain processes en route to decisions and actions. We'll start by looking at biblical principles and relating them to business concepts. My hope is that this will help you see the interrelationships between God's economy and the world's as you strive to serve God's economy even while you live in this world.

Many biblical principles of God's economy are well-known, but we fail to apply them in our business lives. Today's business culture directly opposes some and simply ignores others. And not all of the business principles in the world's economy are bad; many are just not kingdom-oriented. Here's a good example of the contrast:

The last will be first, and the first last. (Matthew 20:16)

The main goal of every athletic race is to be first; competition is usually good and certainly part of human nature. To turn this upside down and put others first is unnatural in our daily business behaviors. But if we are to thrive in God's economy, we answer to a different master.

Here's another example:

Gaining the whole world but losing your soul.

The world's business climate pushes us to achieve everything we can and to make as much money as possible, without stopping to realize that it may come at the expense of our souls. We are influenced by the world's standards to accomplish and accumulate, without realizing that our well-being—the peace and joy that we most desire—comes by seeking what is best for us eternally.

The fact that God's economy is upside down from the world's does not mean that everything is in conflict. Everything in the world's economy is not necessarily evil, because it still bears the mark of the Creator. The big difference is that *all* of God's principles are true and good. Individuals who settle for the world's economy will be pursuing what may not last.

Pursuing accomplishments and making money are not inherently evil, but the outcome of our accomplishments and the use of our money make a world of difference. Self-centered and narcissistic accomplishments are opposite of the humble businessperson serving others. If all money is consumed or hoarded rather than shared with those in need, then satisfaction will forever elude the longing soul of those who accumulate it.

That said, God's economy and the world's economy are often in tension with each other, like the epic battle between good and evil. Think of the world-based economy as an eroding cliff of moral business standards. The erosion results from the rejection of absolute truth. Without absolute truth as a benchmark, the cliff of moral standards sloughs off into an ocean of uncertainty.

Nothing disturbs the soul more than a lack of definite boundaries and benchmarks. We were created to have truth as our bulwark to stabilize our thinking and subsequent actions. So without truth to guide our decision-making, the world's business values vacillate dramatically. The shifting of moral standards in business is much like wind-driven sand. Only when we are firmly anchored in the bedrock of God's principles can we be stabilized and have true comfort for our souls.

Principles for a Successful Business

Jesus taught with clarity the principles that establish his economy. They are incredibly simple, yet astonishingly profound. The genius behind these principles is unfathomable, just as God's nature is hard to comprehend. I love how his words really rock the world's boat. What he said over two thousand years ago still applies in business today.

Below I list several biblical principles that describe God's economy (along with their Scripture references). Each one is followed by a corresponding business concept. This is not a comprehensive list, but it shows how to see biblical principles within a business context. And it will help you build a successful business within God's economy.

Biblical principle: Do for others as you would have them do for you (Matthew 7:12; 19:19; 22:39–40; Mark 12:31; Luke 10:25–28). When we love others as ourselves, we will do for them as we wish they would do for us. This is expressed numerous times in the Gospels, showing the importance of placing others before ourselves. It is inverse to our normal reaction of selfishness and self-preservation. As an example, in our firm we believe that what is best for the employee is also best for us as an employer.

Business concept: Deference. Doing what is best for others is known as deference. *Deference* also means "a courteous regard for others" and "a disposition or tendency to yield to the will of others."[1] We seek to give preference to others by doing what is in their best interests. Showing deference to others is an expression of love toward them.

Biblical principle: The first shall be last, and the last shall be first (Matthew 19:30; 20:16; Mark 9:35; 10:31, 44; Luke 13:30). This is self-explanatory and inverse to how we normally think. Jesus was again expressing the importance of humility versus egotism or narcissism. Those who push to be first on this earth may not be those who are important in eternity.

Business concept: Preference. Allowing others to choose first or to go ahead of us, thus giving priority to others. *Preference* also means favor shown to others over yourself.

Biblical principle: The greatest shall be least, and the least shall be greatest (Matthew 20:25–28; Mark 10:42–45). Jesus used this phrase numerous times with his disciples to explain the importance of humbling yourself and serving others, especially when in a position of leadership. God will exalt those who willingly humble themselves, but he will abase the prideful.

Business concept: Inverse reality. Those who will be important in eternity may not be recognized while on earth. Prideful or self-serving individuals fail to realize the eternal importance of humility and serving others.

Biblical principle: Whoever wants to be great must be servant to all; the leader is the one who serves (Matthew 20:26; 23:11–12; Mark 9:35; 10:31, 43–45; Luke 22:26; John 13:4–5; 13:12–16). If someone wants to be a leader, he or she must serve everyone around him or her. Jesus exemplified this leadership by serving not only his disciples but also everyone with whom he came into contact; Jesus' service for all humanity culminated in his death on the cross.

Jesus gave us the greatest example of servant-heartedness when he washed the disciples' feet. If we are to be like Christ with a servant's heart, then we must willingly perform the lowliest of jobs to serve others. Jesus calls us to serve everyone around us by doing even the smallest things without credit.

Business concept: Service. Everyone enjoys being served. There is real value in serving others, because it blesses those being served. Most clients respond positively to good service and want to continue doing business with those who provide it. *Service* also means "the action of helping others or an act of assistance to someone."[2]

Biblical principle: The humble will be exalted (Matthew 23:11–12; Luke 14:7–11; 18:14). We do not need to exalt ourselves in front of others; rather, we will be exalted if we are humble. Therefore, we do not need to self-promote.

Business concept: Humility. Being self-effacing paves the way to controlling our ego and pride. By remaining humble, we give others the opportunity to recognize our character and actions as noteworthy. *Humility* means "a modest view of one's own importance."[3]

Biblical principle: Greatness in the kingdom of God is humbling yourself like a child (Matthew 18:1–4). The disciples frequently asked who would be greatest in the kingdom of God. Jesus pointed to children, suggesting that their humility was viewed as greatness in God's economy.

Business concept: Childlikeness. Possessing the childlike attributes of trust, obedience, and innocence is not a weakness but a demonstration of faith in the Master of all business.

Biblical principle: You must lose your life to save it (Matthew 10:39; 16:25; Mark 8:35; Luke 9:24; John 12:25). You will save your life if you lose it for the sake of Christ. This is the direct opposite of the way the world thinks. Christ said that pursuing things of eternal value, even at the cost of your life, will bring you true life.

Business concept: Sacrifice. Many sacrifices will be required of those who seek to glorify God in their earthly business life. Sacrifice is "an act of giving up something valued for the sake of something else regarded as more important or worthy."[4]

Biblical principle: Gain the world but lose your soul (Matthew 16:26; Mark 8:34–36; Luke 9:24–25). Jesus asked, "What good is it if we gain everything but lose our souls?" If we sell out to the world, we may accumulate much on earth, but we will retain nothing in eternity. Pursuing riches to become wealthy is like chasing after a mirage in the desert. The destination appears to be wonderful, but the reality will always disappoint. Wealth used in God's kingdom to glorify him is not a mirage but a reality; it will be greatly rewarded.

Business concept: Contentment. Being content with what you have regardless of the amount is a jewel in the kingdom of God. Gain, no matter how large, will never satisfy without contentment.

Biblical principle: The measure you use will be measured back to you (Matthew 7:2; Mark 4:24; Luke 6:38). The way we express our generosity is by giving to others. This generosity will come back full circle to us. Give to others as you would want to receive.

Business concept: Generosity. Giving generously to others with their best interest in mind will eventually bless you in return. Who does not like a generous person?

Biblical principle: Everything grows in God's kingdom (Mark 4:26–34). Many of the parables are agricultural in nature, with the results showing growth. Everything grows, from the small mustard seed to the seed that was thrown into the fertile soil. The parables promote growth and increase. As a parallel, good stewards can be identified by looking for the growth that surrounds them. Everything that is entrusted to a faithful steward will increase for God's glory and kingdom.

Business concept: God-ordained growth. Things grow because God causes them to grow. We will experience growth or increase as we follow his principles and receive his blessing.

Biblical principle: What is highly valued on earth is detestable to God (Luke 16:15). The things of this earth seem shiny, but they cannot compare to what God has in store for us in heaven. God sees both and has assured us that our eternal rewards are more valuable than anything we can have on earth.

Business concept: Kingdom value. God clearly shows his value system in the Bible. The evil in the world battles against God's original design for humanity's success, but carefully mining gems from Scripture will develop a kingdom portfolio.

Biblical principle: Do for others who cannot repay you (Luke 14:12–14). Jesus encouraged us to do good for others, even if they do not repay us. He used the example of inviting the poor to a banquet with full knowledge that they cannot repay. We know that if we lend to the poor, God will repay us.

Business concept: Uncompensated kindness. God will give us eternal rewards for our actions on earth. Serving those who cannot repay will yield large dividends.

Biblical principle: The amount is not the issue in God's kingdom (Mark 12:41–44; Luke 21:1–4). The poor widow in the temple was an exemplary steward in God's kingdom because she gave all she had. The amount she gave in comparison to others was insignificant by the world's standards, but it was extremely significant to God. She is immortalized because of her generosity and love toward God.

Business concept: Kingdom quantities. Because we cannot clearly see God's value system on earth, it is through a dim glass that we understand the measure God uses in his kingdom. The faith demonstrated by the giver has more currency value than the gift itself.

Biblical principle: If you are faithful in little, you will be faithful in much (Matthew 25:21; Luke 16:10; 19:16–17). Being faithful in everything we do is important in God's kingdom. Jesus taught that our stewardship in the little things reveals how we will steward the big things; those who prove faithful in little will be entrusted with more. Faithfulness even in the smallest of instances will yield great rewards at the right time.

Business concept: Faithfulness. Few traits in our character impact relationships more than being faithful. Violations of trust often cause irreparable damage. Faithfulness in the minutiae builds great trust.

Biblical principle: To whom much is given, much is expected (Luke 12:42–48). When we are given wonderful opportunities, we should make good on them. Just as we work diligently to honor a superior's trust in the workplace, so we ought to bring God a significant return on his investment in us.

Business concept: Accountability. When we are entrusted with much, much will be expected from us. An explanation is always required to justify the actions of those who have been entrusted with assets or possessions.

Conflict with the World's Values

These principles for doing business in God's economy may be familiar, but many of them conflict with the world's business philosophies and strategies. If we apply these principles in our conduct at work, the world will recognize us as distinctively different; we will be the light on a hill that Jesus talked about.

With this overview as a foundation, we can delve into the deeper layers of God's direction—the characteristics of his righteousness and how we both demonstrate them and develop them through real-life actions. When we reflect God's character in this way, we honor him and build truly successful businesses.

3

GOD'S BUSINESS
THEME

Several years ago, I was introduced to two young talented brothers hoping to establish their feature filmmaking career. If you know anything about investing in movies, then you know that it's a little like swinging for the fences, accepting significant risk for the chance to hit a homerun. You see the potential in something yet to be proven in the marketplace, and you fund its opportunity to become profitable. Sometimes you lose everything, but one or two good ones can erase your losses and win the game.

Before I tell the rest of this story, I want you to recall our theme of love in business so you can see it in action as it plays out in the story. Jesus' parables frequently portray the Golden Rule as a standard for us to apply in how we deal with others. And it's the theme that undergirds business in God's economy. It simply means to love others by doing what is best for them.

Unfortunately, simple is not always easy, especially when it goes against our natural instincts. We usually need a makeover of our internal operating system to do what is best for others in our business dealings.

Contract Negotiations with Young Filmmakers

I can't tell you the *whole* story because it's still unfolding, but I can tell you what has happened so far. And I can tell you what I'm learning through the process.

These two brothers have been making short films and videos in the commercial film business for over ten years. They've stuck with it, and they've learned a lot about their craft. They've paid their dues, but making commercials and music videos is not where their hearts are at. They want to do something bigger, something with more cultural impact. They want to make feature-length films that will influence their generation.

After meeting them, Marydel and I were infected by their enthusiasm. They were passionate and confident. More importantly, we shared a similar set of values and a desire to communicate truth in a life-changing way. We bought into their vision with our heads and our hearts.

If this had been just another investment opportunity, the answer would have been no because of the risks. But this was different because of the kingdom potential. Along with two other investors, we jumped in with high hopes that this new open door would develop and mature as my work with Walmart had.

Our investment, along with their expertise and hard work, resulted in a feature-length film. The good news was that we now had a quality product. The bad news was that we needed much more than a product. A quality product doesn't do any good sitting on a shelf. Most unproven filmmakers focus on expressing their talent through creating what they love. What they typically do *not* love is finding or making a market for what they create—the distasteful work of getting someone to buy it.

Distribution, along with advertising in the movie business, is a key component to developing an audience. Most young filmmakers focus on making what they hope to be a good film, leaving distribution as an afterthought. Our first film got caught in that trap. Our filmmakers, unknown and without a distributor, had no studio to release their first movie for a theatrical performance. This meant no audience, no sales, and no income. We were at a standstill.

The standstill became more serious as time passed and cash flow became an issue. Our filmmakers needed income to survive. That's when they approached me with a proposal for investment capital, offering me a hefty interest rate and ownership as a partner in their business. This would be a whole different animal from simply investing in a single project; this would raise the stakes—both the risk and reward—considerably.

On a Friday afternoon, we met with our lawyers in my conference room to talk about how we might develop a formal business relationship. Their first offer on the table was for me to loan them enough capital to operate the company for several years. I am not divulging numbers here, but if you think through the annual financial needs of families and a filmmaking business and then multiply the total by five, you'll come up with an educated guess. And you'll most likely guess too low. But on the upside, they offered a 20 percent interest rate and 50 percent ownership in their company. It sounded like the perfect *Shark Tank* opportunity.

I thought hard about their offer. It could mean losing a

bunch of money, but it could also be a great success. But then I looked at it from their perspective. I understood the intensity of their desire to succeed. I also understood that they were underestimating the issues that would inevitably arise if we ended up being successful. They would have given up half of their future profits to a business partner not actually involved in the operations of the company. They might be able to live with that for a year or two, but before long it could become a matter of serious resentment. And the interest rate of 20 percent, if not paid quickly, would compound into an astronomical burden.

Sitting in the meeting, my attention was divided for a while. Part of my brain tried to process the ongoing discussion while another part was thinking, *What would I want if I were in their position? I would want freedom to exercise my best judgment; I would want to be financially unencumbered; I would want wise counsel from experienced businesspeople when storms appear.*

I interrupted the conversation with a counteroffer. "How about this?" I said. "What would you think of a simple interest loan of five percent? I don't want fifty percent of your company; I think it would be better for you to keep it. And I'll allow you to pay the note over a five-year period without having to make payments for the first two years. This will give you freedom to operate within your area of expertise, reduce financial pressure, reward you well if you are successful, and give you access to my counsel when needed. How does that sound?"

I expected cheers, but I was met with silence. The brothers looked at each other, eyes wide, and then at their lawyer. Their lawyer, frozen, stared at me in disbelief.

I finally broke the silence. "What do you think?" I asked.

"I like it, of course," their lawyer said. "At least the first part of it. I'm still waiting to hear the hook."

Such an offer may sound too good to be true because no bank or investment banker would ever consider making it. In fact, if you were bold enough to ask for it, they would laugh on their way out the door. But for these young men to flourish, they needed a long runway to build a profitable company. They had neither the cash nor the ongoing income to make the immediate payments that any bank would require. And how discouraging it would be to be strapped with an unfamiliar partner as the largest shareholder of the company, especially one who was ignorant of the movie industry.

I offered these terms because I knew it would take time to get their business off the ground. I believed in them: their talent, their diligence, their integrity, and their faithfulness. We consummated the deal under my terms. From my perspective, that was in their best interest, and I trusted that God would protect what I intended to be an act of love.

I don't prescribe this kind of offer as a solution for many situations. It's just one example of my attempt to apply a biblical principle as a business concept, think through the corresponding characteristic of righteousness, and then decide on actions that would both demonstrate and further develop that characteristic. In this case, the principle was the Golden Rule: Do for others as you would have them do for you. The business concept was deference, giving preference to the best interest of others.

Oh, in case you're wondering what happened next in the story of our filmmakers, stay tuned. I'll update you in a later chapter.

The Golden Rule

Most of us learned the Golden Rule in grade school or Sunday school. My grandmother posted it in her house. For centuries it has permeated American culture. But many of us disregard it in business. I was not thinking about the Golden Rule when I began researching and writing this book, but I quickly realized that it is the most powerful and transformative theme for operating a business. In fact, it is so important that the New Testament constantly refers to it.

It first appears in the Sermon on the Mount where Jesus taught, "So in everything, do to others what you would have them do to you, for this sums up the Law and the Prophets" (Matthew 7:12 NIV).

The Selfless Love of Jesus

Jesus selected twelve men to intimately follow him during his three-year earthly ministry. He named these disciples as apostles. With the falling out of Judas, Mathias was selected by the other apostles to replace him. Jesus later appeared as a voice from heaven, calling church-persecuting Saul to become church-planting Paul, the thirteenth apostle.

Of these thirteen, four wrote about their experience of walking with Jesus. Matthew and John wrote what later became two of the Gospels—historic accounts of the life of Jesus. Peter and Paul wrote letters to the followers of Christ to encourage them.

John was known as the beloved disciple who had a close friendship with Jesus. Both John and Peter were in Jesus' inner circle, accompanying him on especially notable occasions such as the transfiguration and the resurrection of the dead. Matthew wrote from his perspective as a reformed outsider. Although

Paul did not have the opportunity to walk alongside Jesus while he was on earth, God used him as the most prolific New Testament writer.

These four writing apostles all emphasize the importance of love as exemplified by the life of Christ. Matthew and Luke do it in their Gospels: Do for others what you want them to do for you (Matthew 7:12); love your neighbor as yourself (Matthew 19:19; Luke 10: 27).

The parables found in the Gospels help explain the selfless love of Jesus. They exemplify his love for his disciples, for those with whom he came into contact, and ultimately for all of us. Love was such an important theme, because it led Jesus to lay down his life for our best interest. One of his last instructions for his disciples was to love one another. He told them that by observing their love for one another, the world would know that they were his followers.

Beyond the Gospels, Paul taught that the aim of most of Christ's teachings was to love others, and Peter wrote that the root of the gospel was love.

The Golden Rule Expressed through Love

When Paul, the great theologian, wrote to the Philippians about how they ought to imitate Christ's humility, he made a bold statement reinforcing the Golden Rule. Paul said, "Let each of you look not only to his own interests, but also to the interests of others" (Philippians 2:4). This was Paul's interpretation of the Golden Rule.

Finding it to be a powerful and transformative key to operating successfully, Paul echoes the Golden Rule numerous times in his writings:

- Romans 12:9–10: Love your brother with sincerity; honor others above yourself.
- Romans 13:9–10: Love your neighbor as yourself.
- 1 Corinthians 10:24: Seek the good of others.
- 1 Corinthians 16:14: Do everything in love.
- Galatians 5:13–14: Love your neighbor as yourself.
- Philippians 2:3–4: Consider others as more important and look out for the interests of others.

Writing to the Romans, Paul said that their love must be genuine and that they were to love each other sincerely as brothers and sisters. He wanted to encourage the Roman church to operate in an attitude of love, exemplifying the Golden Rule that Jesus taught. He emphasized that all the commandments "are summed up in this one word: 'You shall love your neighbor as yourself.' Love does no wrong to a neighbor; therefore love is the fulfilling of the law" (Romans 13:9–10).

In his instructions to the Corinthians, Paul encouraged the church to look out for the other guy and to do what is beneficial for him, not just to think of themselves. He also encouraged them to do *everything* out of a motivation of love, confirming that even the Old Testament was based upon this.

When teaching the Galatians about freedom, Paul instructed them to use their freedom to serve one another in love. He continued by quoting a form of the Golden Rule, "The whole law is fulfilled in one word: 'You shall love your neighbor as yourself'" (Galatians 5:14).

As Paul neared the end of his life, he gave instructions to his beloved disciple Timothy. Usually what you tell someone right before you leave is extremely important, especially if you will not have the opportunity to see him or her again. It is the most important thought you want remembered. Paul used this strategic moment to reinforce in Timothy that the main aim of everything he does should be love. He was instructing Timothy to remember that the most important principle in dealing with others was doing what was in their best interest.

Paul sums up his letters by encouraging his readers to do what is best for others while loving them deeply. In so doing, he was reinforcing what the Gospels said about love and reiterating what Christ taught. As he gleaned the Golden Rule from his study and examination of Jesus' life, he taught it to those he pastored.

What Is Best for the Other Person in Real Estate?

Another example of upside-down thinking illustrates the Golden Rule being applied in business. Imagine a property seller lowering the price already offered by a buyer. Who does that? And why? I had never heard of such a thing being done before. And I would have had trouble believing it if I hadn't been there to see it firsthand.

Crown Financial Ministries owned two contiguous buildings that were used as their offices. A local medical group wanted to purchase one of these buildings to expand their adjacent medical facilities. They had previously made offers to buy, but Crown's board of directors had always declined, because the timing hadn't been right for Crown to sell. Until now.

I was on the board when Crown contemplated the transaction. We asked ourselves, "What would be in the best interest of the purchaser of this building?" Since we had delayed the medical group's opportunity to purchase, we wondered what we could do to benefit them.

Sellers typically negotiate the terms and conditions along with the price to benefit themselves. Routine self-interest. We wanted to be the exception by practically applying the Golden Rule. So we asked ourselves, "What does the purchaser really need out of this deal?"

This question began the process of looking at the medical group's offer in light of what was in their best interest. Although they needed a commitment to be able to purchase the building for their expansion, they didn't need to occupy it immediately. We saw a potential win-win in the making. We lowered the price and gained the ability to stay in the building until we were ready to move. The medical group got the property for future use as they wanted, and we received fair compensation for the building in a no-hassle closing transaction.

The Root of Love

Everything in the Gospels seems to grow out of the root of love. Business in God's economy is rooted in the first and greatest commandment to love God with all our heart, soul, mind, and strength. As Jesus went on to explain, the second most important commandment is like it, that we should love our neighbor as ourselves. Jesus clearly states this command to love in Matthew 22:39 and Mark 12:31.

By deduction, I conclude this to be the undergirding theme for conducting business. I do not believe that we can separate our business and personal life when it comes to integrity in dealing with God's commands. Therefore, the root of love in the Gospels is the great commandment for both our personal and business lives.

Peter restated the Golden Rule when he implored, "love one another earnestly from a pure heart" (1 Peter 1:22). We are to love with a pure heart and with great concern—not only for our family and friends, but also for all with whom we deal in personal and business affairs. We do this so that we might ultimately encourage them to believe the gospel.

Peter made a profound statement near the end of his life. He said that we are to "be self-controlled and sober-minded for the sake of [our] prayers. Above all, keep loving one another earnestly, since love covers a multitude of sins" (1 Peter 4:7–8).

Why was this so important to Peter? He had walked intimately with Jesus and heard firsthand his teachings regarding the Golden Rule and the importance of loving others. In their last recorded conversation, Jesus told Peter to love and tend his sheep. Imagine how that conversation branded on his heart the importance of loving others.

4

EXPRESSIONS OF LOVE IN BUSINESS

I endeavor to love those with whom I work by doing what is in their best interests. However, that doesn't mean I ignore what is in my best interest; I just don't focus solely on it. One example of this was when I transitioned my firm's leadership to faithful employees.

Initially, I didn't have a business partner; I felt like I had everything under control and didn't need one. After twenty-five years of operating the firm, I recognized a plateau; I needed additional leadership to bring beneficial change and establish new growth.

Leadership Transition

Giving up ownership—even partial—of a business you've spent your life building isn't easy. The more successful it's been, the harder it is to let go. I knew that a transfer of leadership was inevitable and that I couldn't transfer leadership unless I transferred a real sense of ownership too. The question was how to find the right balance.

I had been advised not to give up control, particularly with unproven partners. When we began the transition discussions, I was planning to sell only twenty to forty percent of the firm to my new partners. This would allow me to observe their steward-ship of the firm, and if they proved faithful, I would give them the opportunity to buy more.

However, transferring this minority percentage of owner-ship would not communicate to them a true ownership in the firm. In my way of thinking, it was the difference between mow-ing the grass "you own" versus mowing the grass "you rent." If I desired an effective leadership transition, then the partners must feel ownership. They needed to hold the keys. Thus, the idea of selling eighty percent of the firm to two younger partners began to germinate in my mind.

We spent months working through the transition details, and I ended up selling eighty percent of the firm to Shade O'Quinn and Larry Craighead. They were tasked with taking the firm's leadership reins, and they received the benefit of real ownership, including a majority of the profits for their efforts. Many of my business acquaintances didn't understand the decision. Some even called me crazy for selling eighty percent of the firm to unproven partners. But I believed it was best for the company, the employees, and my new partners. And if I was right, it would end up being best for me too.

I didn't immediately take the money and retire, choosing instead to stay and help them become successful. This wasn't entirely altruistic; I wanted this transition to work so I would be paid for my stock. But I also had an unselfish desire to see them succeed as the true leaders of the firm. My aim was to do what was best for them, giving them the opportunity to lead and to accumulate wealth for their families while furthering God's kingdom by their generosity. Feeling that God had allowed the company to be blessed, I wanted to steward our profits well. And I believed this leadership transition would allow these men the opportunity to increase their own stewardship.

My selfish side was insecure at times with such a large transaction. My faith side was confident, and I was secure, knowing that I had heard the Lord's whispers regarding the plan. The firm grew even more than we anticipated, which was a true blessing for all of us. In the ten years that have elapsed since the transition, the firm's profitability has increased enough to enable my partners to pay off the stock indebtedness sooner than planned.

Because I did what was best for my partners, they in turn blessed me by sharing profits with me well beyond my percentage of ownership. Since our initial transition, we have brought on two younger partners. You might have guessed it—we sold them a majority share of the firm. This might seem crazy to some, but once again we felt it was best for them, for our employees, and for our clients.

I have stayed on to help this second transition succeed; besides, I enjoy the people and the work at the firm. Yes, it was emotionally difficult to give up ownership of the firm I founded, but these four outstanding, faithful men deserved the opportunity to own it and to take great care of our people.

The Best of Business Partnerships

Business partnerships can be great or a nightmare—few are in the middle. Eventually, they tend to go to one side or the other.

So how do I do what is best for my partners? How do I show them concern? I have learned to do several things.

Retiring partners typically withdraw from burden-bearing leadership once they have sold their ownership in the company. Realizing that a good leadership transition did not mean abandoning my successors, I determined to encourage them and backstop their efforts. Offering unconditional support and bearing burdens alongside them became an act of loving concern.

In the past, I had been guilty of saying, "I wouldn't do it that way, but I guess it's okay." This is not supporting; rather, it's undermining. I quickly learned in the transition that undermining the new leadership was not in anyone's best interest.

Nothing is more important to my partners' success than my support as the founder. Sometimes I feel my partners far exceed what I could have ever hoped to do alone; other times I feel that they are walking on my beautiful Persian rug with their muddy boots. But I know I have a vacuum cleaner and no real damage has been done. Most of my flinches come from a mere difference of opinion, and I'm learning to step aside and allow them to walk on my rug so they can exceed my abilities. It is in their best interest for me to stay with them in a burden-bearing capacity, engaging with them on difficult issues and being willing to get involved with messy or hard decisions.

I also help my partners through encouragement. Shade became president of the local chapter of the American Institute of Architects (AIA). I encouraged him to work within the organization to provide leadership. The AIA recognized him as an excellent leader and promoted him to president of one of the largest chapters in the United States. I was proud of his accomplishment and supported him by attending as many AIA meetings as possible.

Offering solid counsel while remaining with my younger partners demonstrates a loving concern both for them and for the firm. Thinking through unforeseen issues and unintended consequences can be fatiguing, particularly at the higher levels of firm management. So many things in business are unclear, and directing the ship in fog through the reefs is mentally demanding and emotionally draining. The captain must make the right final decision when the pressure is highest, when the ship is heading toward the reefs or a sand bar. Partners with the same burden-bearing capacity make these decisions much easier.

Using human relational capital for the benefit of others is best for our partnership. There is a temptation to keep relationships such as banking, legal, investment, and accounting to oneself in order to increase perceived value or remain indispensable. But introducing and promoting my partners in these relationships is an act of concern for their well-being. By sharing these developed relationships with my partners, I set them up for future business success, which is in everyone's best interest.

I strive for integrity in all my expenditures within the firm. My honesty with credit card use is an important place to start. I do not charge anything that my partners would disapprove of or that I would be ashamed to show them. I buy only those necessities that benefit the firm and avoid little personal luxuries that many businesspeople justify as business expenses. I do not take long expensive lunches or business trips that combine sightseeing excursions and charge them to the business.

I pursue opportunities to assist my partners with personnel. When carrying a heavy workload as they are, identifying areas of weakness becomes difficult, so I observe and assess the weaknesses that need to be addressed. Sometimes, it takes looking at personnel in a unique way, reversing critical roles or adjusting positions that the employee might find challenging. It may require seeing beyond the individual's current job tasks to his or her potential and then suggesting changes to the partners.

I know I am successful when my partners exceed my abilities and employees look to them for inspiration and affirmation.

The hardest task as a partner is terminating employees. Making these employment decisions is difficult, but each partner must be able to fire the people he or she hires. Some partners are not strong in this area, while others have no problem with it.

When I consider the ramifications of firing an employee, it is gut-wrenching. Even when a firing is merited, thinking about the employee's loss of income and benefits with the potential of continued unemployment sickens me. But the willingness to stand with my partners in the arduous chore of terminating employees is critical in helping them bear this tough emotional burden.

After selling most of the stock in the firm I had founded, it might have been easier to simply leave. But staying was the right thing for me to do, enabling me to support my partners and help them succeed. And staying has been a pleasure. Our partnership works because of our willingness to bear the burdens of the firm together while doing what is in the best interest of one another. I have benefited far more than I imagined; I never envisioned how far beyond my expectations they would take the company.

We are not always a perfect partnership, but our desire is to show deference to one another and to demonstrate our love by bearing each other's burdens. This is required for success in God's economy.

Expressions of Love in Business

Every act of Jesus was an expression of his love for others. He was compassionate to everyone and excellent in all he did. Jesus willingly touched the untouchable and engaged in service even when he was fatigued and distracted. Whether late at night or early in the morning, he was willing to get dirty with people. Jesus' extreme love for those he served is an example for all of us to emulate.

Because of this sacrificial love, he gave up everything, including his life, for us. This is the ultimate fulfillment of love in action. We should aspire to Jesus' example by sacrificing ourselves for those we lead. We should willingly sacrifice to protect, provide, and care for those around us. The ultimate display of our love for those we lead is making sacrifices for them.

5

DEVELOPING RIGHTEOUS CHARACTER

WHO WE ARE TO BECOME

Doing and Becoming

As I contemplated what is truly enduring, I realized that righteous character is one thing that can be brought into eternity. Treasures are transported to heaven through the redeemed heart of those who love and abide in Christ.

A relationship exists between doing good things that bear good fruit and becoming men and women of righteous character. The relationship between doing and becoming goes in both directions, just as a door in a commercial kitchen swings both ways. Our actions that bear fruit develop our righteous character; moreover, our righteous character motivates us to perform deeds that bear fruit.

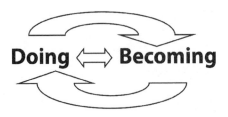

Righteous Character in the Sermon on the Mount

Could you operate your business in God's kingdom if the only Scripture you had ever been exposed to was the Sermon on the Mount (Matthew 5:1–7:28)? I believe so. I theorize that the character traits of godly businesspersons are summed up in the Sermon on the Mount. Such people are characterized by humility, brokenness, meekness, decisiveness, and selflessness. They are recognized as being merciful, honest, good, and peaceful. They are men and women of integrity who make the right decisions, have mercy on others, and are honest when no one else is looking. As much as possible, they are at peace with everyone.

Bearing the Fruit of Righteousness

Bearing the good fruit of righteousness is the outward expression of a person's righteous character. Jesus said that every good tree bears good fruit and that a bad tree bears bad fruit. A good tree cannot bear bad fruit, nor can a bad tree bear good fruit. Thus, a person's character will be known by the fruit that is produced from his or her life (Matthew 7:17–20).

A good person will bring forth good deeds out of good treasure stored in his or her heart. In contrast, John the Baptist told the Pharisees, "Even now the axe is laid to the root of the trees. Every tree therefore that does not bear good fruit is cut down and thrown into the fire" (Matthew 3:10). As with trees, people

DEVELOPING RIGHTEOUS CHARACTER

are known by the fruit produced from the abundance of their hearts.

Mile Markers of Righteous Character

How do we know if we are bearing the fruit of righteousness and becoming men and women of righteous character? There are several indicators that reveal whether we are on the right course. Although the journey takes our lifetimes, it is encouraging to know that we can identify mile markers along the way.

Seeking God's Kingdom

One of the first mile markers I saw as a young man was learning to seek first God's kingdom and his righteousness (Matthew 6:33). Seeking God's kingdom first meant subjecting everything else to that main pursuit. In the Sermon on the Mount, Jesus told us to seek first his kingdom with the promise that he will give all other necessary things to us. Other things may seem important at the time, but seeking them should not be our highest priority.

Money Should Not Be Our Master

Second, as a businessman, I found that it was critical to separate my heart from my money. I could not allow money to be my master, because it would prevent me from effectively serving God. Matthew 6:24 says, "No one can serve two masters, for either he will hate the one and love the other, or he will be devoted to the one and despise the other. You cannot serve God and money."

Separating our hearts from our money is painful. The rich young ruler standing before Jesus faced this dilemma. Zacchaeus faced a similar choice when Jesus asked him to come down out of the tree, telling him that he would stay in his home. While the rich young ruler sadly walked away from Jesus, Zacchaeus chose God as his Master and proclaimed that he would give half of all he owned to the poor and restore fourfold to others whom he had cheated.

Unlike Zacchaeus, the foolish farmer who built larger barns did not separate his heart from his wealth. He was not rich toward God but rather hoarded, keeping all his prosperity for himself. He could not tear his heart away from his money and thought he could take life easy by eating, drinking, and being merry. After declaring his intent, he died later that night because of God's judgment upon him.

In Mark's Gospel, Jesus makes a great point about money. He asks, "For what does it profit a man to gain the whole world and forfeit his soul? For what can a man give in return for his soul?" (Mark 8:36–37). Why does humanity strive to gain all this world has to offer? Rich people desire more riches; powerful people desire more power. The world system drives humanity into further accumulation, thus feeding the egos that make it hard to humble ourselves and submit to God. The lust of the world is the enemy's greatest allurement and tool to keep men and women from seeking God's kingdom.

We are trained and rewarded by the world's economy to pursue more. Jesus posed the question: Even if you were to gain everything this world has to offer, would it be worth the expense of your soul?

Lest we jump to a wrong conclusion, let me point out that wealth in and of itself is not bad; it is the *love* of money that is the root of all kinds of evil (1 Timothy 6:10). Wealth is a great asset if used properly for God's kingdom. We can utilize money to do significant things that glorify him and promote his kingdom; we can use it to serve as the hands and feet of Christ.

Storing Treasures in Heaven

As we labor, we should not lay up treasures on earth, but rather seek to store our treasures in heaven. Matthew 6:19–21 encourages us: "Do not lay up for yourselves treasures on earth, where moth and rust destroy and where thieves break in and steal, but lay up for yourselves treasures in heaven, where neither moth nor rust destroys and where thieves do not break in and steal. For where your treasure is, there your heart will be also."

Nothing is more important in my business than understanding why I accumulate and store my assets. If it is simply for myself, or if I fear that I will not have enough in the future, then they will be subject to the earthly perils of thievery, devaluation, inflation, destruction, and loss.

In 1987, I learned a valuable lesson. The stock market hit an all-time high that year. I thought to myself, *I don't see how things can get much better.* So I took my stocks and bonds and converted them into cash. In October of that year, the stock market crashed on what immediately became known as Black Monday. I miraculously saved my assets because I had converted them into cash near the peak of the market. Although I can't claim that it was because of my financial prowess, I can say that I learned a valuable lesson during the crash: there is no safe place on earth to store our money.

In case you skated quickly over those last few words, let me repeat them, because they form a foundational truth that must be acknowledged if you have any hope of experiencing real success. There is *no safe place on earth* to store our money.

If I trusted in the stock market, it was subject to wild market swings. If I put it in a bank, I was subject to bank failure, which happened to numerous banks later that year. I could have put it in gold or commodities, but then I risked the commodities market tanking. I could not find a place that could guarantee the safety and security of my assets.

That's when I realized what Jesus was saying in this passage. If we put our treasures in heaven, no one can take them away and they will not be devalued or lost. So Marydel and I began our journey of storing our treasures in heaven. It has been a life-long effort, but as we do so, our hearts follow those assets and investments.

How do we store treasures in heaven? If we examine the context of the command given in Matthew 6:19–21, we see that it comes on the heels of three admonitions: giving to the poor and needy, praying, and fasting. Then the context returns to the subject of money, reminding us that we cannot serve both God and money. I'll address this issue more in the final chapter.

Persecution of the Righteous

If you follow God's principles, you may well be persecuted in business. Worldly business practices and politically correct ideology may not align with godly principles. This is particularly evident in the political arena as we observed during the last presidential campaign. Many business practices allow greed and corruption to permeate the business culture. Unfortunately, the world will eventually persecute those who have righteous character. The world's standards and political correctness are at odds with these characteristics.

I want to make a careful distinction here. Many of our truly righteous actions *will* be appreciated by the world, particularly those related to the Golden Rule or the fruit of the Spirit. They often result in an advantage for us even in the world's economy. Other righteous actions, however, will not result in the world's applause or affirmation. When we take a stand against any ungodly thing, we offend someone's private kingdom of evil. Any time we shine a light into the darkness, the forces of darkness fight back.

The evil of the world will oppose anyone known for righteousness (Matthew 10:22). Satan, the current ruler of this earth and the one behind this persecution, will be defeated at Christ's return in his great reckoning. I am so thankful for this victory and that those with righteous character will eventually be blessed by inheriting the kingdom of God. Their rewards will be in heaven, never to be stolen, lost, or destroyed.

The Epic Battle between Love and Hate

Just as we will experience persecution for being righteous, so we will also be hated without justification. We should not be surprised or fearful, because Jesus predicted, "And you will be hated by all for my name's sake. But the one who endures to the end will be saved" (Mark 13:13). This means that representing Jesus and his kingdom is likely to make us hated at times by the natural business world. So we should buckle our seatbelts and not be surprised when persecution comes. This is a result of the epic battle between love and hate, the same battle between good and evil that has existed since the beginning of humankind.

Sin and the brokenness of our world have resulted in the proliferation of hate. Worldly hate lurks in every false religion. As we look around the world, we see many places where evil triumphs. But we should not fear or lose hope, as Jesus has overcome the world and given us the means to bring goodness in his kingdom. Jesus went on to encourage us not to be fearful, for there is nothing the world's evil can do to our souls.

The principles in the parables are used in the fight against evil. That is why it is so important to develop righteous characteristics as armaments to fight against evil and the missiles of hate. The number one secret weapon at our disposal is love.

The Lifelong Journey

How will we know what mile marker we are on? I think it will be signified by the type of fruit we bear at the time. Matthew 12:33–35 reminds us that the tree is known by its fruit. The good person, out of the good treasure stored in his or her heart, brings forth good deeds for God's kingdom. That is an indicator of moving along the path of becoming a man or woman of righteous character. We never reach the end of this challenging journey during our lifetime, but mile markers along the way encourage us as we produce fruit of growing quality and quantity.

For Further Study

- Matthew 6:19–21: The heart follows the treasure.
- Matthew 6:24: We cannot serve both God and money.
- Matthew 6:25–32: God's great provision.
- Matthew 6:30: Seek first his kingdom.
- Matthew 12:33; Luke 6:43–45: The tree is known by its fruit.

- Matthew 13:23: The great harvest.
- Matthew 19:16–22; Mark 10:17–23; Luke 18:18–29: Story of the rich young ruler.
- Luke 12:13–21: Story of the rich foolish farmer.
- Luke 19:1–10: Story of Zacchaeus.

6

ACTIONS THAT BEAR FRUIT

WHAT WE ARE TO DO

Earlier, I shared the importance of developing a heart of righteous character. This character defines our soul and who we are to become as men and women for the future. We have the privilege of developing this character while we are alive on earth. But as eternal beings, we transport this character into God's kingdom as we work to glorify him.

But righteous character does not just happen. We develop it through a lifetime of engaging in right actions. Though we do not like to talk about it, the heart contains both good and evil within it. Originally, I did not believe that good and evil coexisted within the heart, but as I have come to know my own nature and the pull of sin's temptation, I realize that I have done things that do not make sense to my kingdom mind-set.

While reading the parable of the weeds that were sown in

the field, I began to understand this dilemma of coexistence. In this parable, Jesus said that an enemy had come and sown weeds among the good wheat in the field of a farmer. Good wheat and bad weeds began to grow together. At harvest time, the weeds were removed and then the crop was harvested. Likewise, when both good and evil coexist in my heart, it doesn't mean that my heart is totally bad; the weeds just need to be removed.

I can relate to the apostle Paul's struggle, the battle between good and evil within his heart:

> For I do not understand my own actions. For I do not do what I want, but I do the very thing I hate. … So now it is no longer I who do it, but sin that dwells within me. … For I do not do the good I want, but the evil I do not want is what I keep on doing. … Wretched man that I am! (Romans 7:15, 17, 19, 24)

In Jesus' death and resurrection, God delivered us from the penalty of sin and freed us from slavery to sin. The battle between good and evil will continue in our hearts, but we know that the battle has been won in Christ, so we can persist in pursuing hearts of righteous character.

The Battle for Our Hearts

The battle for a person's heart was illustrated when Jesus asked his disciples, "But who do you say I am?" Peter replied, "You are the Christ, the Son of the living God." And Jesus said, "Blessed are you, Simon Bar-Jonah! For flesh and blood has not revealed this to you, but my Father who is in heaven" (Matthew 16:15–17). This revelation reflected God's goodness in Peter's imperfect heart.

Immediately after this confession, however, a great battle ensued inside Peter. When Jesus predicted his death, Peter took him aside and rebuked him, " 'Far be it from you, Lord! This shall never happen to you.' But he turned and said to Peter, 'Get behind me, Satan! You are a hindrance to me. For you are not setting your mind on the things of God, but on the things of man'" (Matthew 16:22–23).

The apparent inconsistency between Peter's confession and the rebuke of Christ was due to the great struggle in his heart. In spite of his good intentions, evil was attempting to blind him to the goodness of God's plan. We know that eventually goodness won out as the keys of the kingdom of heaven were given to Peter and the Christian church was built upon his faithfulness.

It is only through abiding in Christ that we can overcome the evil and allow good to permeate our souls. Righteous actions are required to develop righteous character. But if our lives are void of the Holy Spirit's influence and we do not abide continually in Christ, we will never develop into men and women of righteous character. As Jesus explained, "I am the vine; you are the branches. Whoever abides in me and I in him, he it is that bears much fruit, for apart from me you can do nothing" (John 15:5). If we desire to experience true kingdom success, we must pursue good deeds and righteous character through abiding in Christ and submitting to the Spirit.

Swinging and Revolving Doors

The relationship between character and actions is two-way, like the swinging door in a commercial kitchen, but it is also like a revolving door in the front of a building. At a solitary moment in our lives, we can do a good deed that moves us forward in developing righteous character (this is like going through the swinging door). But if we rest on our laurels, we can miss the intended exit and backslide into unrighteousness (this is like going around and around in a revolving door in which our sinful nature traps us). In this fallen world, righteousness does not make a one-way entrance into our soul. We must maintain our pursuit of righteousness through continually abiding in Christ, allowing sanctification to be accomplished within us.

Righteousness developed through fruitful deeds is critically important. James, the servant of the Lord and the brother of Jesus, said it well:

> What good is it, my brothers, if someone says he has faith but does not have works? Can that faith save him? If a brother or sister is poorly clothed and lacking in daily food, and one of you says to them, "Go in peace, be warmed and filled," without giving them the things needed for the body, what good is that? So also faith by itself, if it does not have works, is dead. (James 2:14–17)

In other words, what good is it to wish a person to be warm but not give that person a coat? What good is it to wish someone to be well fed but not feed him or her?

The story of Jesus' life on earth is filled with his righteous deeds. Jesus never talked theoretically about righteousness or theologically about actions; rather, he spoke practically about how to develop righteous character through our actions. Jesus was a man of action, and the multitudes perceived his character to be righteous through his actions. We too are to be righteous men and women of action, pursuing fruitful deeds.

What I endeavor to do in this book is combine the

characteristics of the righteous man and woman with the actions that bear the good fruit of those characteristics. It is difficult to separate characteristics from actions when looking at the holistic picture of life. The more we do, the better we become, and the better we become, the more we do. By bearing good fruit, we prove that we are Jesus' disciples.

Each of the following chapters is titled with a characteristic of the righteous person and a subtitle as a word picture or memorable phrase. Within each chapter, specific actions that bear fruit are highlighted in the text. I have attempted to embolden specific, concrete actions that both manifest and further develop righteous character.

The bold actions in the chapters to follow are far from exhaustive. They are merely examples from my own experience in business, as well as an occasional example from someone else. My hope is that these few examples will help you make the connection between righteous characteristics and actions that bear fruit in your own life.

In this upside-down world where we naturally tend to accept the deceptions of satan, it is often difficult to see where our current decisions are leading us—what future we are creating for ourselves day by day. I urge you to train yourself in decision-making by constantly posing two questions:

1. Will this action bear fruit that belongs in God's kingdom?
2. Will this action develop in me the righteous character of God's kingdom?

Please use my examples ahead as springboards for creating actions that bear fruit in your own business, career, and home life.

7

LOVE AND COMPASSION

DEMON-POSSESSED PIGS

Jesus had compassion on the great crowds as he looked out upon them. He had compassion on the sick, the weak, and the demon possessed, not to mention the rich young ruler as he asked Jesus a thoughtful question. Jesus had compassion on the crowds even when he was busy, distracted, and fatigued. Because he loved them, he made time for them, honoring them by meeting their needs. Jesus embodied love and compassion in daily life.

First and foremost, as business leaders operating in God's economy, we should be known by our love and compassion. As emphasized earlier, the most important undergirding business principle is that of loving others by doing what is best for them. We set the example of being different, being the salt of the earth and the light of the world, just as Jesus taught. Nothing shines brighter than esteeming those around us. Being created in God's image, all men and women deserve honor, and we express love by following Jesus' example, thus honoring all men and women by serving them.

In a similar way, when we love and pray for our enemies, we are obeying what Christ taught us. Similarly, Proverbs 25:21–22 says that if you feed your hungry enemy or give him water when he is thirsty, then the Lord will reward you. Not only is it a command to love your enemies, but there is a reward for being obedient to do so.

Three Loves of Business

In my many years of leading our firm and other businesses, I have learned that there are three loves to develop. As a professional, I have learned to love what I do. As a service provider, I have learned to love my clients and customers. And as an employer, I have learned, at times through my failings, to love my people.

Loving what you do enables you to work diligently and to do what is necessary to be successful. If you love what you do, you have no trouble staying late or coming in early to work.

Serving my clients became easier when I learned to love them. Learning this love has taken many years, but I have devoted myself to getting to know and to love working with my clients, thus making it easier to continue serving them when they are difficult or demanding. Love and selfless service go hand in hand.

I have endeavored to love my employees in a selfless manner. I pursue what is best for them, and I believe that what is best for them is also best for our firm. If they have unique needs, I try to meet those needs or provide a different opportunity within the firm. If I think it is in their best interest to resign and move to another employer with a different opportunity, then I support them in that decision and bless them as they depart.

When I interview new employees, I repeatedly comment that I really do love the people who work here. I have learned to love our people in such a way that not only do they enjoy their positions, but they also feel secure working in our firm. The fact of the matter is that I have learned to deeply care for them. This love does not come naturally, but it can be developed.

As business owners and leaders, we should have compassion on everyone, just as Jesus did. This compassion is best demonstrated to our employment family when we work with them in an understanding and loving manner. An employee was fired from our firm recently. Initially I might have resented him because he did not perform well and took advantage of us, but the Lord reminded me not to repay in kind. He had been dishonest with his accounting of time, working on personal projects during office hours, but I needed to be compassionate. I had to stop myself from being critical and resentful in how I handled the situation. Yes, he had wronged our firm with his complacency and selfishness, yet my being angry or curt with him was not appropriate or helpful. Yes, we needed to be firm and decisive as employers, but we also needed to act with kindness and compassion.

Loving those whom our firm serves and those who serve our firm makes it easier to take excellent care of both. I have urged our leaders and my business partners to learn to love everyone outside of and within the firm. An effective way to do this is to pray regularly for each client and employee.

By developing these three loves, we have a great formula for providing wholehearted service not only to our clients but to our own people as well.

Compassion on the Crowds

Jesus was often inconvenienced by the multitudes surrounding him, yet he maintained composure, having compassion for those in the direst of circumstances. Even as he grieved over the loss of his cousin, John the Baptist, he had compassion on the crowds that came to him because he understood their situation as harassed and helpless; he said they were like sheep without a shepherd.

I have caught myself becoming irritated when I'm interrupted in the middle of a busy workday, but I have realized that when people in the office approach me, their concern is important to them. To show compassion and consideration, I have learned to stop what I am doing and to focus on them by looking up from my table. As a business leader, it is important for me to give them this time to assist them, even if it is an interruption.

I learned this principle by observing how Jesus handled the many interruptions and inconveniences from those who crowded around him. Yes, embracing interruptions might make us inefficient in our work, but being attentive and focused serves those around us well. In the long run, we accomplish much more by helping and working through people than we could accomplish on our own. Listening to people in their time of need, although often an inconvenience, is central to making them feel important and loved.

Jesus went through all the towns and villages of Israel preaching the good news, and when he saw the crowds, he had compassion on them (Matthew 9:35–36). Jesus often withdrew to solitary places, but the crowds followed him. When he saw them, he served them, healing the sick and meeting their countless needs.

A phenomenal example of Jesus' compassion was when he encountered a demon-possessed man who lived among the tombs on the far side of the Sea of Galilee (Mark 5:1–20). While others had sought to bind the man with chains and shackles, leaving him to cry out and cut himself night and day, Jesus relieved him of his torture by casting out the debilitating demons and sending them into a large herd of pigs. Filled with gratitude for the compassion Jesus showed, the restored man immediately asked to follow him. Jesus responded by telling him to go home and share all that had been done for him.

Jesus traversed all of Israel and loved all those with whom he came into contact. He boldly loved and healed the untouchables. No greater love has ever walked this earth. The culmination of his love was his death in our stead on the cross. It is hard to comprehend this kind of love, a love that willingly died for the very enemies who crucified him.

Jesus talked constantly to his disciples about loving one another, and in his last admonition to them, he said, "By this everyone will know that you are my disciples, if you love one another" (John 13:35 NIV). We too can make the world take notice by loving those around us and by having compassion on our employees and customers. After all, showing love and compassion was how Jesus lived his life.

For Further Study

- ◆ Matthew 9:35–36: Jesus had compassion on the crowds.
- ◆ Matthew 5:1–20: Story of a demon-possessed man.

8

SERVANT HEARTEDNESS

PICK UP THE PAPER TOWELS

I love the example Jesus set on the last night he was on earth. He stripped himself of his outer garments, grabbed a bowl of water, knelt before his friends, and began washing their feet. This was considered the lowliest of jobs that only a servant would perform. Although Jesus was King, he served his disciples and all of humanity in this act of humility. His ultimate servant heartedness was demonstrated in his willingness to pay the price for humanity's sin the next morning through his sacrificial death. Jesus told his disciples that the Son of Man came to serve, not to be served (Mark 10:45).

In the three years prior to that night's historic event, Jesus walked as a servant among the poor and disenfranchised. He healed them, cast out demons, and fed their bodies and souls. He touched the deplorable lepers and ministered to widows and children. He associated with society's worst sinners—the tax collectors, prostitutes, money changers, and even lawyers. In his willingness to spend time with these people, he met their deepest physical needs and gave them hope.

Jesus served the multitudes by feeding them on multiple occasions. In two recorded events, he miraculously fed a fantastic number of people. At the feeding of the five thousand, a number which included only the men in the crowd, it is estimated that as many as fifteen thousand people were fed when including women and children. Everywhere Jesus went, he met not only physical needs but also the greater spiritual needs of people's souls. He satisfied their thirst with the living water of his salvation.

In our firm, we exercise servant leadership by living out the belief that no one is too good to perform any task. All our leaders and managers should be willing to cheerfully perform any task they ask of subordinates. This includes helping with filings and distributions or staying late to check drawings and write specifications.

Knowing that the best leaders are those who serve those around them, we use the phrase "pick up the paper towels" to illustrate servant leadership within our firm's culture. The illustration came from the paper towels that are always lying around on the bathroom floor. No one seems to want to pick them up; instead, they leave it to the cleaning crew or a janitor, which means the paper towels lie around all day. When a leader sees the need and picks up the paper towels, he or she exemplifies a servant's heart, meeting a need without receiving credit.

No One Is Too Good to Do It!

As I learned how Jesus served, I began to look for ways to serve my clients, employees, partners, and outside vendors and contractors. Small tangible acts of service can be effective in expressing genuine love.

A simple thing I did for our new employees was to shampoo the carpet around their workspace in our design studio before they started. When we hired a new employee, I would shampoo the carpet around their area so that it was nice and fresh before they arrived. I would usually do it early in the morning so no one would see me. On other occasions, I have snuck into the breakroom to take the dishtowels home to wash or to wipe down the counters. These simple acts help me fight against my pride and become more servant-hearted.

Over time, I noticed our servant-hearted culture took root. It became contagious with many employees who began wiping the counters after they were done. Now when I go into the restrooms, no paper towels are lying on the floor. Our people are picking up the paper towels to ensure that the restrooms are clean for the next person. This is a small but tangible way we are learning to serve one another.

I noticed my business partners are usually the ones who clean up after we have a company potluck luncheon. I also have noticed my partners straightening up the seminar room after a continuing education event. Those simple acts of service go far in developing a culture of servant heartedness.

On the Other Hand

Employees who profess a faith in Jesus should not take advantage of employers. I have noticed that some Christians within our firm have been disrespectful, while some have treated me more like a brother than an employer. Sometimes there tends to be a casual nature between Christian employees and their bosses, but Christians should not take advantage of their employers, just as employers should honor and take good care of employees. Christians should serve their bosses all the more because of their love for God and the knowledge that they are working for the Lord rather than for people (Colossians 3:23–24).

Never Be "Put Out"

As an expression of servant heartedness, we should never be "put out" by a request. Always respond in a positive manner. Do not act "put out," as my mother would say; rather, joyfully help with any request. This is especially important when serving our clients.

Many times, our clients call at inconvenient times asking for last-minute changes. Occasionally they ask for the impossible to be done in the time allotted. But when serving clients, it shows real servant heartedness to respond in a positive way, thus giving confidence that you will meet their needs. Nothing speaks louder than a positive and cheerful response to a client's desperate request.

The same goes with our employees. When they ask something of us as managers or owners, we should cheerfully respond by giving them our full attention. Most employees are encouraged when their leaders place them as the highest of priorities by immediately responding to their needs. Nothing kills relationships faster than when we feel we have inconvenienced someone with a request. We have all experienced that at a service counter in a store or at a restaurant when the server ignores us.

I have always thought it easier to serve our clients if we first learned to love them. I have made it a practice to get to know and love my clients. It is so much easier for me to attend to their best interest if I have learned to truly love them.

A unique way to serve our clients is to look for ways to make their jobs easier, to make them successful within their own companies. After all, it serves our best interest to make our clients look good. Often, they will pass the credit on to us, but even if they do not, they know that we are the ones who really helped them accomplish a challenging task.

Giving Clients What They Need

When serving clients, I find it best to give them what they need and not only what they ask for. Sometimes the client thinks he knows his needs, but we might know that something more needs to be done. We serve our clients by not just doing the minimum of meeting their expressed need but by also giving them our best.

In the mid-1990s, I was asked to attend a meeting in our client's corporate office. During that meeting, they shared that they had a problem with inconsistent construction specifications. This client constructed numerous projects using the same design and format. But each project seemed to be built under different standards. The design manager had written a list of specifications and requirements in a notebook format. He would photocopy the list of specifications and give it to contractors, expecting them to build it.

He requested my help in reformatting this information to appear more professional and to ensure consistency among the projects. From his perspective, he was simply asking me to clean up his notes and reformat them.

After examining the task, I recognized that it would be more complex than he thought. To accomplish their goal of consistency for the long haul, the specifications for remodeling their projects would need to be in a standardized format recognized by both the architecture and construction industries.

I set out on a mission to rewrite the specifications to be professional, clear, and understandable to the construction industry. This was more than he had requested, but I knew it was what needed to be done. I worked diligently to present a thorough set of construction specifications for the remodeling of these projects.

Upon review, the client realized that this was what they needed and that we went far beyond their initial request. As a side note, these specifications have been used again and again for over twenty years. All projects completed since that time have been constructed using our master specifications.

Take the Middle Seat

No one seems to want it because that is the way we have been programmed. When flying on Southwest Airlines, you can choose your seat, any seat, so long as someone is not already sitting in it. I have noticed, in my many years of traveling on Southwest, that the middle seat (the one between the aisle and window seats) always fills up last. Last-minute travelers routinely get stuck there.

What does this have to do with servant heartedness? In the kingdom of God, servant heartedness usually entails doing what is best for other people. Taking the middle seat not only shows servant heartedness but also enables us to have double the impact on the people around us. Most folks like the room of the aisle or the comfort of looking out the window and leaning against the wall, thus perceiving the middle seat to be undesirable. But there are advantages to taking the middle seat:

1. You do not get bumped by the drink cart.
2. You do not get cold from the window.

3. You only have to ask one person to get up to go to the lavatory.
4. You can take advantage of all three overhead lights and the benefit of two air vents.
5. You can make two new friends at one time.

I appreciate Gary Kelly, the president of Southwest Airlines, as he always takes the middle seat when he flies on one of his own airplanes. You can tell Southwest Airlines was built on service, and it is that servant heartedness that shows through, even from the top.

Serving Our Employees

In serving our employees, we look for ways to be attentive, helping solve problems quickly and being proactive to meet their needs. Putting off or avoiding our employees communicates a lack of interest or concern. Nothing encourages employees like an attentive boss who actively engages in their work and assists them with problems. Simply being present, engaged, and available is the beginning of service to our employees. Absentee leaders who are not available as resources to employees can create dysfunction and isolation within the team.

Checking in with our employees on a consistent basis allows them to feel important and part of the team. I love cruising the office, speaking with each employee daily. It is my hope that my visits encourage them and that they see my interest in them not only as professionals but also as friends.

Serving My Partners

I shared earlier about loving my partners by doing what is best for them. I have attempted to serve them since the beginning of our partnership. When we executed our leadership transition, I was motivated to transition the ownership of our firm as well. It was my opinion that you cannot transition leadership without transitioning the ownership too; it was not my attempt to get out from underneath the firm, to avoid the pressures and liabilities, or to take the money and run.

My motive was to help the firm flourish under new leadership. The only way I knew to do that was to mentor faithful employees who would be able to continue and expand the stewardship of our firm. It is much like the concept that Paul shared with Timothy—entrust to faithful people who will be able to entrust to others (2 Timothy 2:2).

I applied this stewardship principle to our leadership transition. But to transition effectively, I felt I needed to stay with my partners to help them in the transition, so I remained as a subordinate partner to help them become effective leaders among our employees. I went from chief executive to vice president, backing up and undergirding the majority partners. I elected to stay with them to serve them in any way possible so that they could successfully lead our firm and serve our employees and clients. I found real joy in staying with my partners.

The Ultimate Example

After James and John arrogantly requested of Jesus that one of them sit on his right and the other on his left in the kingdom, Jesus replied, "Whoever wants to become great among you must be your servant, and whoever wants to be first must be slave of all" (Mark 10:43–44). Servant heartedness is key to being first in God's kingdom and within his economy. This is upside down from what the world says, but we are to be followers of Christ's example as a true servant to all those around us.

The epitome of Jesus' love and servant heartedness is seen in him washing the twelve disciples' feet at the Passover supper. This washing was a sign of supreme service, the ultimate display of servant heartedness. As our Lord and teacher, Jesus set the example for us to follow, and to do so, we must look for ways to humbly serve those around us. A servant is humble and not greater than his or her master, according to Jesus.

The mark of a Christian businessperson is his or her humble love for others expressed through service. The example set by Jesus washing the disciples' feet means that as leaders we should be willing to do any task we ask of our subordinates, and we should not ask anyone to do something that we are not willing to do. Therefore, serving others is an important principle for operating a business within God's economy.

In John 12:24, Jesus taught that a grain of wheat must fall to the ground and die if it is to produce more. If we die to ourselves first, then we can serve Jesus and others, thus following his selfless example. Humbly dying to ourselves will allow us to better love Jesus and serve others, resulting in a new life that honors God.

Jesus did not come to be served, but to serve and to give his life for many. He explained that whoever wants to be great must become the servant and whoever wants to be first must become a slave. Greatness means servant heartedness. To be first in God's kingdom, we must be such a servant.

For Further Study

- ◆ Matthew 20:25–28: Whoever is great must serve others.
- ◆ Matthew 23:11–12: The greatest will be the servant.

- Mark 9:35: For anyone to be first, he or she must be a servant.
- Mark 10:43–45: Whoever wants to be great must be a servant.
- Luke 22:26: A leader is one who serves.
- John 13:12–16: Jesus washes his disciples' feet on his last night.

9

FAITHFULNESS

WHEN NO ONE IS LOOKING

Over ten years ago, I was struggling with a project to design a children's village for the orphaned and vulnerable in Zambia. I solicited the help of numerous young interns in our office to design the facility as a pro bono project. Since most work was done after hours, none of them made the extra effort to stay late and work on it. They did not understand what was necessary or engage with the project as I had expected.

One Friday evening, I shared with my partner, Shade O'Quinn, that I was disappointed in the effort given by these young, talented architects. I thought this was a great opportunity for them, but they did not embrace it at the level I had hoped. I left frustrated. But when I arrived on Monday morning, sitting on an easel in my office was a beautifully designed auditorium building. Without my asking, Shade spent the weekend design-ing the most efficient and effective project for these vulnerable children in this poverty-stricken country. It was a beautiful design that was eventually built. Literally tens of thousands of orphans have benefited from this wonderful building. The fact that my partner came in after hours to design this building, when no one else was looking, was a wonderful testimony of faithfulness.

My partners have been faithful to me. They go way beyond the norm, making special efforts to ensure our firm's success.

Jesus Was Always Faithful

He who is faithful in little will be faithful in much. Jesus taught this principle unambiguously. We are not going to be faithful with the big things unless we can show our faithfulness in the little things. God's upside-down economy is like that, contrary to people's natural inclinations.

Jesus was faithful in the smallest of details, as exemplified by his returning the donkey to its rightful owner after he rode it into Jerusalem on Palm Sunday (Mark 11:2–3). Throughout his life, it is undisputable that Jesus was faithful in all that he did. He not only taught about faithfulness but also demonstrated faithfulness to his disciples, his most intimate friends. They could not stay awake and keep watch for him on his last night in the garden of Gethsemane, yet he remained faithful to them. Even when his closest companions abandoned him, he faithfully fulfilled his mission by going to the cross, rising from the dead, and encouraging his friends to follow him for the rest of their lives.

When No One Else Is Looking

As Jesus was talking to a crowd, he told the story of a faithful and wise servant. This servant was doing all the things he was supposed to do, even when no one was looking. Though his master had gone away, leaving him unaccountable, the servant faithfully executed his duties. When the master returned unannounced to find his servant faithfully serving him, he entrusted the servant with much more (Luke 12:42–44).

I find that to be true with my employees too. I have numerous employees who do just enough to get by when no one else is looking. I also have faithful employees who, when no one is looking, will "stay late to make up for coming in early." They are faithful regardless, because intrinsically they want to serve and do an excellent job. They exemplify what Jesus was talking about with the faithful servant.

Lisa, my personal secretary, does many things for me when I am out, everything from making sure that calls are properly handled to responding to important correspondence. If I am traveling, she works in the evenings if necessary to ensure that I get home safely. Many early mornings she has checked me in on flights to ensure that I have a reserved seat. I appreciate how Lisa takes care of me, because her faithfulness exceeds that of her job description. Her faithfulness is shown in doing what is necessary to help me become successful, even when I am not looking.

Examples of Faithful Stewards

In the parable of the ten minas, there were faithful and unfaithful stewards (Luke 19:11–27). Jesus used this story of stewardship to communicate the importance of faithfulness. A nobleman gave ten servants a mina each, which was equivalent to fifty shekels or 1.25 pounds, probably of silver, instructing them to put the mina to work during his absence. Upon his return, the master required each servant to give an accounting of how he handled his mina. The first servant brought not only his mina but ten additional minas. The second brought five more. The master commended both servants, saying, "Well done. Because you have been faithful in a very small matter, take charge of much more."

A similar parable has the same application (Matthew 25:14–30). In this story, the master gave three servants talents to manage. A talent was approximately seventy-five pounds, a large measure of probably gold or silver. He gave one steward five, another two, and the last he gave one talent. Two of the stewards were faithful as they doubled what had been entrusted to them. The last servant was lazy, bringing back the solitary talent to his master without having done anything with it. The master called him *unfaithful* because he took the talent and buried it. Why did Jesus call the first two men *faithful*? It was because they knew what was required by the master and worked diligently to meet his expectations. The lazy servant hid his talent out of fear, believing his master to be hard, and he was not faithful to invest it as the others had.

In the same way, we are entrusted with our clients' projects. Our clients have expectations and many times are hard on us. But when we provide services that meet their needs and exceed their expectations, we are like the stewards who doubled their talents. Once our clients find us faithful in what they have entrusted to us, they reward us with more work, just as the master rewarded his servants. The greatest reward for our faithfulness is our clients' affirmation when they find out that we have diligently worked extra hard for them.

One time a senior vice president of Walmart decided to audit our travel expenses, taking our invoices and carefully examining them. Travel expenses are the smallest portion of the costs we pass on to Walmart, and we have hundreds of projects each year that require travel. Travel could be done in a careless way and expenses submitted that might benefit the traveler, but our firm's culture is to treat Walmart the way we want to be treated. So we spend as little as possible for the benefit of Walmart.

That is what the senior vice president of Walmart told us after doing a thorough examination. He said, "I thought that RHA was faithful, but looking at the small expenses of travel, I know that they are because I did not find any expenses that were out of line or exceeding the allowance." We were found faithful when no one was supposedly looking, yet they were looking. In fact, they were looking carefully at what we were doing.

This helped our reputation at Walmart, and, as a result, we were rewarded with more work in subsequent years. I do not attribute our workload just to this one instance, but it certainly convinced the client that we were faithful when no one else was looking.

If we are not faithful in what is entrusted to us, then who will entrust us with true riches? If we are unfaithful with other people's money, who will give us our own? This is an additional motivation to diligently take care of our clients.

No one may ever find out what we do, but if we are caught doing good things and not bragging about them, our faithfulness will serve our best interest in the future. I also know that if we do the wrong things, then it could result in the opposite—it could ruin our reputation and sever a relationship.

Faithfulness with Others

Faithfulness with people is more important and harder than faithfulness in our actions. I deeply regret the times I have been unfaithful to people in my life. Sometimes the damage can be irreparable. Hopefully those relationships can be redeemed over time, but it drives home the importance of faithfulness.

Faithfulness to our families is most critical. It has been my experience that most people find it difficult to be faithful all the time in all they do. When no one will find out or when no one is looking, there is a temptation to be unfaithful. If faithfulness is not the highest priority in our personal relationships, then tragic consequences result.

I have been unfaithful in some of my business relationships in the past. It caused pain and disappointment to them—and to me. Faithfulness builds a business relationship while unfaithfulness destroys it quicker than anything else. It is far worse to be unfaithful than to be incompetent. I have seen the damage it can do, and I endeavor not to let it happen again.

We all know the feeling of being betrayed. So faithfulness with my partners is an important attitude and resulting action. I do not want to lose their confidence in me because I am unfaithful to them, even when they are not looking. When it comes to expenses within the firm, I pursue faithfulness, not spending more than necessary and certainly not spending the firm's money on personal items. I strive to spend money in such a way that my partners would be proud of me as a faithful partner to them.

We should always be faithful to those underneath us. We should take up their cause and try to look for opportunities to serve them. I think subordinates sense faithfulness from their superiors. When we are faithful to them, they feel secure and desire to work hard.

My partners and I have sought to be faithful to our employees in their compensation. When our firm makes profits, we share a sizeable percentage of those profits with them. They have faithfully served us by taking care of the client, so we should faithfully take care of them by compensating them. It seems unconscionable to me to keep all the profits. I certainly would not want to be treated that way.

When I think of faithfulness, I think of my beloved springer spaniel, Norman. When I am home, Norman waits at the back door or looks through the windows because he wants to come in and be with me. He is a faithful friend, always happy to see me and forgiving me if I am short or impatient with him. He willingly sits at my feet while I read or watch TV. Norman has taught me a lot about being faithful despite how he is sometimes treated. He is a good reminder to be faithful with people regardless of their attitude toward or treatment of me.

The Amount Is Not Important

The poor widow slowly walked to the offering box and dropped in two small coins, about one sixty-fourth of a day's wages. She did not notice if anyone was looking; she certainly did not do it for show. She just dropped the coins—all she had to live on— to express her faithfulness and love for the Lord. Jesus watched from a distance and said, "This poor widow has put in more than all of them" (Luke 21:3). She was faithful with the little and has been immortalized as one of the most faithful stewards in God's kingdom.

All of Scripture reveals God's faithfulness to us, even though we do not deserve it. That has taught me that I am to be faithful regardless of others' responses to me.

For Further Study

- ◆ Matthew 24:45–46: Faithful and wise servant.
- ◆ Matthew 25:14–30: Parable of the talents.
- ◆ Matthew 25:21, 23: He who is faithful in a few things.
- ◆ Luke 12:42–48: Being faithful during the master's absence.
- ◆ Luke 16:10–12: Faithful with little and with another's property.
- ◆ Luke 19:11–27: Parable of the ten minas.
- ◆ Luke 21:1–4: Story of the poor widow.

10

HUMILITY

BANQUET SEATING

At a recent fundraising banquet for International Justice Mission, I was seated at a prominent front-row table in the grand ballroom. This was neither requested nor anticipated by me, but I have to say it was quite an honor to be seated up front with a wonderful view of the program. It made me recall the illustration Jesus used about banquet seating. How embarrassing it would be to sit in a place of honor and then be asked to move to a lower position!

Jesus said to let others honor you rather than pursuing honor for yourself. In Luke 14:7–11, Jesus uses a parable to demonstrate why humility is important. He said not to take the best seat at a banquet, because someone more important than you may come and you will be asked to move to a lower position. Rather, he said to take a lesser seat so that the master of the banquet will ask you to sit in a more important seat, thus honoring you.

I seek to apply this principle in my business; rather than pridefully promoting myself in front of clients and colleagues, I try to remain humble by taking a lower position and allowing them to exalt me if I deserve it. Whoever exalts himself will be humbled and vice versa.

The principle we are to learn from this parable is to take the lower position and to let others praise you. Your self-promotion will be viewed as arrogance and detested by most. Can you think of people with whom you have dealt in business that have been self-assured, prideful, and self-promoting? I certainly do not enjoy listening to them share about their greatness.

From his humble birth in an animal stable to his humiliating death on the cross, Jesus embodied humility. All of his interactions with people were characterized by humility and compassion, not pride and authoritarianism. The week before his death, Jesus entered Jerusalem on the back of a donkey as a humble Savior, not as a ruling king. And on the night before his death, knowing the cross was imminent, Jesus ministered to his friends by humbly washing their feet as an expression of servant-hearted humility. He set the example of humility for us to follow in serving others.

Humility of Knowing God

Jesus taught his disciples the importance of humility through the parables and in many conversations. The Pharisees and scribes were prideful due to their religious knowledge and stature in society. They thought they had much to be proud of, but Jesus taught that our worth is not in what we know or in our social position, but rather in who we are as we stand before God. If we truly know God, it will humble us.

Humility of a Child

Greatness in the kingdom of God is determined by humility—childlike humility, to be exact. When asked who was greatest in the kingdom, Jesus answered that it was whoever humbles himself or herself as a child (Matthew 18:4). The characteristics of a child that Jesus commemorated are:

- Teachable
- Faithful
- Obedient
- Dependent
- Vulnerable
- Innocent to worldly ways
- Quiet before elders or authorities
- Hopefully optimistic

Humble Examples

Following the Passover supper on their last night together, and after washing his disciples' feet, Jesus instructed them to follow his example, choosing to serve regardless of one's stature. Mark 10:43–45 says it this way: "But whoever would be great among you must be your servant, and whoever would be first among you must be slave of all. For even the Son of Man came not to be served but to serve, and to give his life as a ransom for many."

In the Sermon on the Mount, Jesus said that the poor in spirit will inherit the kingdom of God. I take that to mean that the humble will be those of foremost importance in God's kingdom. Even the Lord's Prayer is a humble supplication to God. Jesus taught us to pray in a humble way, not in cowardice or fear, but in confidence that if we humble ourselves before God, then he will grant our requests.

Jesus often contrasted the proud with the humble. While at the temple, he noticed two men praying. He praised the man who beat his chest saying that he was unworthy, and he exposed the Pharisee who did good and lived religiously but was prideful and self-justified. The humble, broken tax collector—not the Pharisee—went home justified before God. Jesus said that anyone who exalts himself will be humbled, and anyone who humbles himself will be exalted.

On another occasion when Jesus was teaching, he told those listening to humble themselves, take up their cross, and follow him. It is interesting that only a short time later the disciples argued about who was the greatest among themselves. Even those who walked closely with Jesus did not understand the importance of humility at the time.

In one of the most heartfelt stories of humility, Jesus was reclining at a table when a woman known to be a sinner approached him with expensive perfume. I can imagine the scene as she knelt before Jesus, tears streaming down her face. With a deep sense of humility, she repented of her previous sin and lifestyle. She washed Jesus' feet with her tears, dried them with her hair, and then kissed and anointed his feet with perfume. This is an extreme example of humility and generosity. Jesus honored this woman for her humble act, and her story is told even to this day.

In another story, Jesus became aware that power had gone out of him as he walked through a crowd. A woman had humbly touched the edge of his garment, thinking to herself, *If I just touch the edge of his cloak, I will be healed of this infirmity of bleeding*. She was healed, and Jesus recognized her humble act and her faith before the crowd. I marvel that Jesus called her his daughter.

In God's economy, everything seems upside down. The lowly of society, the women, and the children were used as examples of greatness in the kingdom precisely because of their humility.

Personal Humility

For us to be effective as humble businessmen and business-women, we must have personal humility in our lives. This humility comes through a personal relationship with God and an understanding of his magnificence that causes us to realize who we are as mortals. Nothing humbles us more than entering God's presence.

In our firm, I have endeavored to have an attitude of humility toward others. Although from the beginning I have aspired to be an excellent architect, I asked God for two things—one of which was not to be famous. It seems to me that famous people tend to also have the characteristics of self-promotion, egocentricity, and selfishness. I knew that to be important in God's kingdom, I should never have these characteristics in my life. So I asked the Lord to keep me humble, and I worked to avoid self-promotion.

A practical way in which I developed humility was not bragging about my accomplishments to my peers. I chose not to advertise our firm as another small way of keeping humble. So we did not have a website, and I figured that if my work and professionalism were good enough, I would survive by good reputation. That proved to be true as we received most of our work through referrals and repeat clients. I also did not submit for awards and recognition, which is common in the profession of architecture. Most architects jump up and down wanting to be recognized for their creative design talents, thinking this will set them apart from others. I believe that honor is due for all people and that we should be honored for the things we do well, but to self-promote or to seek our own honor is not a principle Jesus taught.

I have also learned to apply the principle of not allowing my deeds to be seen by others so that I might be rewarded by God and not by others. I try to provide service to my clients, employees, and partners in such a way that I quietly practice my righteousness. Jesus spoke against practicing our righteousness in front of others to be seen by them (Matthew 6:1–4). Although our deeds will find us out, whether good or bad, we must not promote our good deeds in hopes of being recognized and rewarded. Jesus taught that when we give to others or when we pray, we should do so secretly, so that we may be rewarded by God later.

Christ did not glorify himself; rather, the Father glorified the Son. Therefore, we should not seek our own glory but let others speak well of us and sing our praises. We are tempted to tell others about what we have done or who we are because we fear that they might not find out. But the more effective method is to wait for others to speak of our deeds and character. Others' praise is more credible than the praise that comes from our own lips.

Corporate Humility

As a firm, we endeavor to express a humble appearance in our physical offices. We have lovely offices in an old historic building; however, we keep our office and furnishings simple. We did not spend all the allocated "finish-out" money on the premises because the space was open, highlighting the original construction. Our desks are made of solid core doors laid on wood bases that we made ourselves; once painted and organized, the place looks quite handsome. When clients and visitors enter our office, they say, "Wow! This is a cool office!" As part of our culture, we aim to remain unpretentious, simple, and prudent to represent our core value of humility.

I have always encouraged my partners to live humbly as well. I found in Scripture that prudence and humility dwell closely together as sisters. So I try to exemplify prudence in my lifestyle, home, and cars. In striving to be humble, I have certainly battled false humility, trying to appear to have less than I really do. That is equally a sin in the sight of God. My wife has been a great balance for me, helping me recognize the times that I am being prideful through false humility.

I certainly do not advocate a need to live in poverty or below an appropriate lifestyle simply because of frugality. The measure is not quality and quantity of possessions, but whether we are living in congruence with how God has blessed and convicted us individually. We sometimes project a false image by striving to appear humble. It correlates closely to the proverb that says there is a person who pretends to be rich but has nothing, and a person who pretends to be poor but has great wealth (Proverbs 13:7).

The greatest way to be a leader for others to follow is to serve humbly.

For Further Study

- Matthew 18:1–4: Whoever humbles himself or herself like a child is greatest in the kingdom.

- Matthew 19:14: The kingdom of heaven belongs to children.
- Matthew 19:30; 20:16; Mark 9:35; 10:31; Luke 13:30: The first will be last and the last shall be first.
- Matthew 20:25–27: Whoever is greatest must be the servant.
- Matthew 20:28: Jesus did not come to be served but to serve.
- Matthew 23:11–12: Whoever humbles himself will be exalted.
- Mark 5:25–34: Woman who touched the edge of Jesus' garment.
- Luke 7:36–50: Woman who anointed Jesus' feet with tears and perfume.
- Luke 9:46–48: The discussion between disciples— who was the greatest.
- Luke 14:7–11: The story of banquet seating.
- Luke 18:9–14: Parable of the Pharisee and tax collector.
- John 8:50, 54: Jesus allowed the Father to glorify him.

11

———
———

SHEPHERDING

HOLDING THE PEN
OF YOUR DESIGNER

Jesus came to earth as the great loving Shepherd to gather his sheep. He called them by name, nurtured and fed them. He did not come to rule over them, but to serve them with compassion. He saw his sheep as lost, harassed, helpless, and in need of a leader (Matthew 9:36).

As leaders, we should follow Jesus' example, loving and shepherding our people well. I frequently tell my partners and managers to "know well the condition of your flocks" (Proverbs 27:23). Although this statement comes from Proverbs, Jesus echoed it in his words and works too. As the Great Shepherd, Jesus expects those in authority to lovingly shepherd those entrusted to their care by knowing them well. Jesus calls us to be shepherds of our people.

In the Middle East at the time of Jesus, shepherding was a

common job. God honored several lowly shepherds by inviting them to see the newborn Christ; they were the first to praise him as Lord and Savior in response to the angels' glorious announcement of the Messiah's birth. Jesus frequently used the illustration of shepherding in his teaching. For example, Jesus commended the good shepherd who would leave the ninety-nine to find the one lost sheep. And when Jesus spent his last hours on earth with Peter, he gave Peter crucial instructions to take care of, feed, and tend his sheep.

Shepherds who owned sheep would diligently care for them, but hired shepherds were less concerned. Hired men would not risk their lives for the sheep, but the shepherd who truly loved his sheep would protect them by fighting off predators, even at risk to his own life. He would feed and nurture them so they would thrive. In the same way, I have encouraged my partners and managers to shepherd our people. They are to nurture our people just as a good shepherd would his flock. And the truth is that we cannot really nurture our people if we do not know them well. So spending time and listening carefully to them is an important charge.

We shepherd our people by giving them a sense of security, having compassion on them, and being interested in their lives. Simply greeting them each day or checking on their work progress may not have the depth of care required of a good shepherd. Although there are appropriate boundaries with all employees, caring deeply for them is important. I try to subtly get to know them, their struggles, and their personal stories while at work. I endeavor not to pry, but I always have a listening ear if they want to share about their personal lives.

As a boss, it is important not to discriminate, harass, or pry into sensitive personal areas, but loving-kindness and true caring will never push those boundaries. I simply ask them how their children are doing or what they are doing over their vacation as an entry point into their story. Careful observation will notice when they are distracted, distraught, or disengaged from their work. We can't make everyone happy or solve their personal problems, but shepherding includes caring deeply at the sacrifice of our daily agendas.

As I know our people, I enjoy them immensely. Everyone has a unique story. "Our sheep" will always sense that the shepherd loves them and will sacrifice for them. I want them to say that they always knew I deeply cared for them as people and not merely as employees.

Being an Excellent Employer

Early in my career, I learned that being a good employer meant being an excellent shepherd and that it was just as important as being an excellent technical architect. So twenty years ago, I made a conscience decision to be a great employer. As a good architect, I had a maximum staff size of twelve. But as a nurturing employer, our firm began to grow. Fluctuating between seventy and eighty architects and support staff, we are in the category of large national firms, but this healthy growth would not have occurred without focusing on being a shepherd to my people.

I endeavor to shepherd my employees in ways that I would want to be treated. No, I do not become a best friend to each of them, but I always seek their best interests. I look for ways to encourage them. Many times, it is with money—a reasonable salary and extra bonuses. I also look to honor them so they feel valued. I try to remember each employee's birthday with a card. I also cultivated a habit of praying for my employees by name on a weekly basis; this intercessory prayer has caused me to develop a deep love for each of them.

We honor them on their employment anniversaries. On an employee's first anniversary, we give him or her an expensive pen to commemorate putting up with us for a year. On an employee's five-year anniversary, we give him or her a commemorative lapel pin: the five-year pin is pure silver and the ten-year pin is pure gold. These expensive pins are one way we show our appreciation.

Giving raises, bonuses, and gifts are not the only ways to show appreciation either. Many employees want affirmation. Walking through the office each day and patting an employee on the back or speaking kindly will encourage him or her. I try to learn the names of most of my employees' spouses and children. I seek to know what is going on in their lives as much as is practical and appropriate. If they are having a rough go, I attempt to be sensitive and encourage them. I try to know what they are doing on each project, enough to know if they are "under the gun." All employees go through challenging times, including sickness, marital conflict, troubled children, and health and financial issues. A compassionate shepherd will sense these and support them as appropriate.

Some employees have needed financial help. Others have needed help navigating the court system or engaging an attorney. Some have had health crises with spouses and needed time off or some other kind of special care. Several have battled cancer, and sadly, we've lost two of them. But while they were with us, we sought to lovingly encourage them by showing compassion and kindness.

Being a good shepherd also means correcting and disciplining employees. We have fired employees because of incompetence, inappropriate actions, or a poor work attitude that affected other employees. Sometimes we have separated the flock so that others are not affected by those being disciplined. We try to discipline in a loving manner, although it may seem harsh to the person at the time. We have not had to fire many employees for violations of office policy. We have had few violent threats exhibited in the firm, but when one employee became hostile toward one of our female employees, we immediately removed him from the office and terminated him. This is all part of being a good shepherd.

Solely being friendly will not give employees security or confidence. I remember my favorite coaches and teachers were not always the nicest and easiest, but they were the ones who provided justice and protection while always being supportive and encouraging.

When I was trying to determine who would be good leaders and future owners versus merely managers, I would subtly give employees opportunities to prove their leadership potential. I remember one evening when there was a water leak from the floor above our office. The water accumulated unseen until it began to drip, endangering our computers. It quickly became serious as water began to pour down from the floor above. One young man we were considering for leadership ignored the leak and walked out the door to go home; that showed me his character. He was not willing to inconvenience himself with that problem late at night.

On other occasions, I have noticed the leaders in our office staying late with their subordinates to help them. If there was a deadline, the leader of that program would stay late, order pizza, and assist and encourage the staff. One of those leaders is now an owner of our firm.

Holding the Pen of Your Designer

If there is anything I have learned in working with talented people, it is not to hold the pen of your designer. I relearned this lesson recently when we had the opportunity to design a playhouse for a charity auction event. I offered the project to all the young interns in our office, and a young man stepped forward. The design parameters were not given by the women's committee of the charity; they simply wanted a playhouse that would be auctioned off during a local home tour. Our intern chose to design a contemporary playhouse.

My initial reaction was that it should be a cute playhouse where little girls would enjoy playing with their dolls. Of course, being over sixty years old, I had my own preconceptions of what was cute. In my mind, it should have been a playful adaptation of a traditional Tudor-style home.

When the intern designer brought his sketches to our first meeting, I hardly understood what he was trying to communicate, even though I am an architect with forty years of experience. My initial reaction—which I kept to myself—was, *That won't work because it's too complicated. The volunteer contractor who is going to build it won't like something this outrageously edgy and possibly expensive to build.* In my mind, the budget should have made use of standard house materials and totaled around two thousand dollars.

Our intern formed a committee, working together with several other young interns. He was the lead designer, and his design was implemented with their help. In our second meeting, he presented a 3D model of a contemporary playhouse that would go along with a contemporary home. Again, I thought in the back of my mind, *What if these thirty- to forty-year-old mothers don't like it? Maybe I need my own plan B design just in case.* He carefully explained his concept and that the design would allow children to participate in the physical structure. Several days later, the design was completed. I was impressed.

It took this lesson for me to regain a bit of wisdom: allow talented people to go forward—with guidance but not interference. I am grateful, despite the temptation, that I didn't grab the pen of this young designer and tell him what to do. I let him work out his creativity and vet the design solution. Although it was not my initial idea, I am proud of his design effort.

In nurturing young people to reach their full potential, I realized I should not impede their creativity. Yes, I might redirect if they go in a wrong direction, but I never want to discourage them. As an architect, it would be tempting to direct, guide, and influence the design, but the fact is that they might have a better idea.

Our clients from the Women's League absolutely loved the design and our presentation. They were so excited that it was creative, contemporary, and appealing to younger families. I learned a lesson right then and there: Trust the young people, help them, and do not get in their way. Things usually work out. Wisdom tells me that we should entrust, supervise, and allow talented people to perform. Don't hold the pen of the designer.

When Employees Leave

In the early years of our firm, I looked at employees as vital assets to the firm. I almost viewed them as possessions to accomplish the firm's work. But as I aged and realized the importance of doing what is best for them, I have learned that God loans us our employees for a season. They are not possessions, and I should have no expectation that they should work for me out of obligation. I need to think about what is best for them.

So when employees voluntarily resign—or even resign in protest—I look at it from their perspective and what is best for them. I have learned to bless them by giving a good reference or assistance in other areas of life, if appropriate. In the past I was sometimes angry at employees who would leave, but I now try to encourage them that they can count on me if they need help or advice.

I also seek to understand why they left the firm. Often, they just want to do something different. But if they have an issue with the firm, I want to know it; I ask them in a kind way to share honestly. Even if they are angry and leave in protest, I humble myself before them to understand my failings as an employer. If the employee has wronged us, we strive to be generous and not vindictive.

Essentials of an Owner in Business

When I was contemplating what makes a good leader and a potential owner of our firm, I simplified the parameters into a few categories. Three essentials emerged: owners must be protectors, providers, and shepherds. Although all three are essential, each is distinctive. Owners of our firm must be able to do all three, but they do not have to be equally proficient or talented in each area. That is one of the strengths of a partnership: the partners come together to form the perfect triangle or balance with the strengths of each partner complementing the weaknesses of the others.

For Further Study

- ◆ Matthew 18:12–14: Story of a shepherd.
- ◆ John 10:1–5, 11–15: Being good shepherds of people.
- ◆ John 21:15–19: Jesus' final talk with Peter.

12

LEAD BY EXAMPLE

JESUS AS THE ULTIMATE EXAMPLE

Jesus set the example for all to follow. In the Gospel of Mark, Jesus' first recorded act was to be baptized by John. He did not need to be baptized for forgiveness of sins, but he humbled himself to set the example for others to follow. John even asked Jesus, "I should be baptized by you, and yet you come to me?" To which Jesus replied, "Let it be so now." He was showing the way.

When Jesus knelt before his disciples at the Last Supper and washed their feet, he epitomized leading by example. He could have instructed his disciples to lead by example, but through this humbling action, he embedded the example of service in their minds. Likewise, my employees are more impressed by what I do than by what I tell them to do.

As Jesus put in long hours to accomplish his mission, he set the example for us to work hard. Even when he was fatigued, he never ceased to meet the physical and spiritual needs of those who came to him. Jesus' work seemed endless, yet he chose to set the example of being diligent and hardworking for us to follow.

When Jesus awoke early to pray to his Father in solitude, he taught us the priority of abiding with God. And on the night before his death, Jesus explicitly taught that we should abide in him, as we can do nothing apart from him. Jesus' rising early to spend time with God is an example that all successful businessmen and businesswomen must follow if they are to accomplish great things for God's kingdom. I can do nothing outside of what God empowers me to accomplish. When I am in tune with his heart, I hear more clearly his direction for me.

I have not always been faithful to get up early or to spend time in solitude or retreat with God. But as I have realized how critical it is to my being a good employer and leader, I have now made it a priority.

Training Others to Do the Work

Jesus worked through his disciples to accomplish his tasks, as seen in the disciples' helping to feed the four thousand and five thousand men. He asked them to have everyone sit down in groups of fifties and hundreds, and after blessing the food, he had the disciples distribute it. The leftovers they collected far exceeded the small amount they started with.

Jesus could have miraculously fed the multitudes alone, but he employed his disciples to accomplish the work, training them for the work of the ministry. We should also train and encourage others in tasks even when it is hard, inconvenient, or messy. Jesus certainly could have performed the miracle without them, but he chose to include them so that they would participate and better understand his ministry. Likewise, our subordinates and employees will better understand our mission if we show them how to do things in lieu of just telling them.

Jesus delegated tasks to his disciples as he sent them out in twos to preach and heal, bringing the kingdom of God to the people. When they returned, they excitedly reported the miracles they had performed. Jesus used the delegation principle of leadership to train his disciples.

Jesus also taught his disciples as he went along the way doing his work. He utilized every opportunity to teach them. As leaders, we should follow this method of training and not rely solely on training seminars or continuing education classes. Through example, we show our subordinates how to do our work.

Setting the Example

Despite having a carefully outlined dress code, our employees still wonder what attire is appropriate at certain times. I often tell my male employees, "If you want to know how to dress in the office, just do what I do. Observe how I dress."

In the Sermon on the Mount, Jesus said that whoever does the commandments of God and teaches others to do so will be great in the kingdom of God. Teaching through modeling, Jesus said, "Follow me; do what I do."

The Pharisees were notorious for telling everyone what to do. They piled regulations and burdens on the congregation, such that it was difficult to live an acceptable life to the Jewish tradition. Jesus criticized the Pharisees for failing to practice what they preached and instructed his followers to not be like the Pharisees (Matthew 23:3). He said to lead by example, not only by words and instructions. The best thing for my employees to see is my consistency. I do what I ask them to do. I do not place burdens on them that I am not willing to carry myself. Leading by example is the only effective way to train subordinates or employees for the long term. Setting the example always speaks louder than words.

Jesus also set the example for us in how he resisted temptation. When satan tempted him at his most vulnerable time, Jesus taught us how to combat the evil in this world. He fought back using Scripture and his knowledge of God's commandments.

Operating a Business as a Light on a Hill

In the Sermon on the Mount, Jesus said, "Let your light shine before others, so that they see your good works and give glory to your Father who is in heaven" (Matthew 5:16). In other words, be an example for others to follow, but do it in such a way that the glory and credit go to God, not you. Being a testimony to God's goodness and morality is like being a light on a hill; we are there so others will see and follow our example. We must remember that we are witnesses not for our own glory but for the Father's.

Jesus also said not to lose your saltiness as a witness of righteousness. Just as salt brings out the flavor in food, so our exemplary actions should bring out the best in those around us, lifting them up and encouraging them to succeed.

Our corporate mission statement says: "To provide the highest quality professional architectural service to our corporate clients, to be Christian in actions and *distinctively different*." Our distinction from others is that we endeavor to be light and salt by setting the example for others to follow.

Practicing What You Preach

Live humbly and do not require of others what you are not willing to do yourself. A good example of leading employees is to stay late with them when overtime is necessitated and to help them in the labor. In the past, we had to work overtime to meet our deadlines for certain projects. Rather than simply asking employees to stay late, I would remain with them to help produce the work, check it, and write specifications. We often ordered dinner to be brought in as an encouragement. I never wanted my employees to stay late if I was not willing to stay with them. Of course, it is impossible to stay late with every employee on every occasion, but setting the example and willingly serving them created our culture of diligence in taking care of the client.

I can think of no better way to lead by example than to sit alongside your employees while accomplishing a common goal.

Example of Abiding

Jesus retreated. His retreats were often for prayer and to abide with his Father. He frequently went alone, but sometimes he took his disciples with him. The purpose was simple—to withdraw from the crowds, to rest, to pray, and to develop relationships. We are told that Jesus retreated many times through his recorded three-year ministry. Seeking the Father in solitude was such a habit for Jesus that it was the last thing he did on earth before he was arrested and executed; he retreated with the Father in the garden of Gethsemane.

We do not know everything Jesus did during these retreats, but we know he taught his disciples by example. He shared with them the intimate things of life and ministry. It was time away from the rigors and patterns of daily life, a special time for renewal.

I have observed the importance of retreating in my own life. It is a time for me to fellowship with God, to love him and seek his will for my life. From the time our staff expanded to more than ten people, the firm's leaders have annually retreated. These retreats have evolved over the years, and many important decisions have been made during these times. They serve as a time to reflect and evaluate where we have come from and where we intend to go; they also give us an opportunity to discuss in depth the important issues not easily addressed in the daily fray of operating a business.

During one retreat in Santa Fe, when I was still the sole owner of the firm, I identified the weaknesses in our firm and decided to solicit what I would later call burden bearers. These burden bearers eventually became leaders, my partners, and owners of the firm. This retreat was an instrumental time because we talked about the issues and the responsibilities of leadership, management, and ownership. Since then, we have taken many retreats to different fun places, combining pleasure with serious contemplation.

Many people want to be leaders. I ask them, in response, to show me their fruit. Matthew 7:15–20 says that we will recognize others by their actions. What example are you setting for others to follow?

For Further Study

- Matthew 3:13–17: The baptism of Jesus.
- Matthew 4:1–11: The temptation of Jesus by satan.
- Matthew 5:13–16: Be salt and light for others.
- Matthew 5:19: Great in the kingdom is one who teaches truthfully.

- Matthew 14:13, 23: Examples of Jesus retreating.
- Matthew 20:28: Jesus set the example by serving and sacrificing for us.
- Matthew 23:3: Practice what you preach.
- Mark 6:30–32; Luke 9:10: Jesus retreating with apostles.
- Luke 4:42; 5:16; 6:12: Example of Jesus praying in solitary places.
- Luke 9:12–17: Story of feeding of four thousand and five thousand men.
- John 15:1–8: Jesus' teaching of abiding in him.

13

WISDOM

AN APT WORD

Nothing is more valuable in a business than wisdom. Wisdom is granted by God, and he is generous to give it to those who ask. The Old Testament book of Proverbs extols the value and virtues of wisdom. A careful study of Proverbs reveals that there is nothing more valuable than possessing it. I define wisdom as simply looking at things from God's perspective.

In the parable of the ten virgins and their lamps, five were wise because they looked ahead and planned. In another parable, the master called two of his servants wise because they took entrusted assets and increased them for their master; he applauded their efforts, saying, "Well done, good and faithful servants." In a third parable, Jesus told about a servant who was found to be faithful upon his master's return; this master also commended the servant for being wise because he took care of those under his charge.

Wise Choices

My business partner, Ty Holcomb, brought a parable to life as a wise person taking care of our client. Several years ago, Ty stood at a National Rental Car counter and made a decision that would affect our firm. Knowing that the Walmart travel policy requires a compact car, he faced a dilemma—take the tiny Fiat 500 subcompact car in front of him or upgrade for no extra charge. Knowing our client, Ty took the Fiat and drove to his meeting.

Thirty minutes later, when Ty arrived at the construction job shack for the meeting, a civil engineer, an attorney, and a Walmart architectural manager laughed hysterically as he peeled himself out of the car. Ty said it looked like a Ringling Brothers clown making a house call. The civil engineer even took a picture of him as he straightened up his clothes.

When the laughter died down, the Walmart representative said, "In all seriousness, I do appreciate RHA. I never worry about their invoices. It's always appreciated." A few weeks later, he assigned our firm three more projects as a direct result of serving the client in this wise manner. Walmart appreciated Ty's complying with not only the letter but also the intent of their travel policies. Ty's wisdom was proven that day by complying even though he was tempted to upgrade his car. He had no idea that he would be watched so closely by our client.

Timely Words

I remember God giving me wisdom for the moment when I needed to make a statement to a potential client in 1984. As it turned out, that statement has served our firm well over the past thirty-four years. I had been referred to a large national retailer, and after several months of silence, a contractor suggested that

I call this company in hopes of obtaining commissions from them. When I called, I asked the design manager if I could provide architectural services for their future projects. He said that he did not have any work to hand out at the time. I replied, "I'm not asking for work right now. I'm looking for work in the future when you *do* have some to hand out."

He said, "Well, that being the case, I will keep you in mind. We normally assign our work later in the year."

That conversation began a relationship with a client that has now become the world's largest retailer. The wisdom to respond that way meant that I would not be immediately discarded as a hungry architect looking for work, but that we would be kept in mind in the future. Later that year, I was astonished to be handed a large group of projects. God gave me the wisdom in the moment to reply aptly. I do not think I would have thought of that on my own.

As the founder of our firm, God has given me wisdom to navigate many reefs in the tumultuous sea of business. Often we do not understand or see problems clearly. In each instance, I knew that I did not have the wisdom on my own and that I must request it from God. It is difficult to captain the boat in a dark sea, particularly when reefs are not obvious. Wisdom is the best companion during those times.

For Further Study

- James 1:5: God gives wisdom to those who ask.
- Matthew 24:45–47: The story of the wise servant.
- Matthew 25:1–13: The parable of the ten virgins.
- Matthew 25:14–30: The parable of the talents.

14

SACRIFICE

WRESTLING PRACTICE

I would wake up on freezing Oklahoma mornings to run along the highway on days I did not have practice, because I had the lofty goal of being a good wrestler. My sweatshirt and pants would be thoroughly drenched in sweat by the end of the run. I also ran during practices because our nationally renowned coach required us to run to Interstate 35 and back. We would then start our two-hour routine of working on holds, practicing moves, and wrestling. The sacrifice was worth it because our high school team dominated our state, and we became known as the toughest team to beat.

Anything worthwhile requires sacrifice. Through wrestling in high school, I learned the meaning of sacrifice from a physical sense. Not only was I required to lose weight to make my weigh-ins, but I had to be in exceptional shape to wrestle nonstop for the six-minute match. Six minutes does not seem like a long time, but when you are wrestling full throttle, it feels like an eternity, especially if you are out of shape. Being in shape required the sacrifice of hours of working out, running, sweating, and dieting. Why did I sacrifice? Because I had the goal of being a good wrestler; I had dreams of dominating my weight class. It was worth it.

Jesus knew his sacrifice for us was worth it because he loved us. Only God could love us to the extent that he would willingly sacrifice himself, experiencing an excruciating death on the cross. But we were worth it to him. He said that he came to die as the ultimate sacrifice not only for those who loved him but also for his enemies. In response to Jesus' sacrificial love, our main purpose on earth is to love God and others as ourselves.

The Art of Sacrifice

We need to learn the art of sacrifice in business. Everything worthwhile requires a sacrifice of time and effort. In building our firm, I sacrificed many long hours away from my family, working in my office alone. Some mornings I saw the sunrise because I had worked all night. There were mornings I would get up at 3:30 a.m. to catch a 5:45 a.m. flight. My philosophy has always been to catch the first flight out to have a better chance of making all my connections. After a full day of inspecting a project, I would fly back late at night, sometimes logging as many as twenty hours in a day. That sacrifice was well worth it because of what I was trying to accomplish. I was endeavoring to build a firm of outstanding quality with excellent service that would one day be an economic engine to help build God's kingdom.

Jesus told about being the Good Shepherd who lays down his life for the sheep. He sacrificed himself to care for his sheep. The hired person lacked that kind of courage, but the shepherd who owned the sheep was willing. We too must sacrifice for our employees as their shepherds.

I don't claim to sacrifice for my employees often, but there have been times when I put their interests ahead of my own. During the Christmas holidays, for example, many employees spend time with their families. Some try to combine vacation along with the office holidays. My policy over the years was to stay in the office during the holiday period so employees could take time off. As the owner of a firm, it's logical to have first "time off" priority. I have always been concerned that taking that approach would be selfish and not serve the employees well. I stay in the office between Christmas and New Year's Day every year. Although the office might be rather docile during that week, I have found it important to make sure the firm runs efficiently with the minimal staff. It might not sound like a big deal, but there is a family sacrifice.

As an employer, I've always felt the burden of taking care of my employee family. Giving them gainful employment (including extra bonuses) is in itself not a sacrifice, but there is an emotional burden I carry to take care of our people. Employees may not sense that same burden of responsibility. As firm owners, our emotions are sacrificed for the benefit of the people.

Sacrifices—Necessary for Success

I meet few young men in our profession who are willing to make the sacrifices necessary to be outstanding architects. But when they do come through our firm, we know that their hard work and sacrifice will eventually be worth it. Most, however, prefer not to sacrifice, being content to do the minimum required. Very few stay to watch the sunrise the next morning.

I have been tempted with our clients to not worry about a project or a deadline. But then I remember that the sacrifice is worth it. Staying late to complete the job or taking that early morning flight is worth it. I have discovered that it is easier to keep a client happy than to find a new one, but it still requires sacrifice.

Without sacrifice, mediocrity and complacency set in, resulting in a deterioration of business and the loss of clients. I realized that continual sacrifice is necessary to keep a healthy firm going. It may be easier to do the bare minimum, but without meaningful sacrifice, we will not continue to paddle up river. And anyone who does not paddle up river will certainly float down. Floating down the river is easy, but fighting to go upstream takes sacrifice. My experiences have proven that the sacrifice is worth it.

For Further Study

- Matthew 27:26–50: Jesus was the ultimate sacrifice.
- John 10:11–15: Story of the good shepherd.

15

OBEDIENCE

BUILDING ON A FIRM FOUNDATION

When Jesus agonized over his impending death, he prayed to his Father to let the cup pass from him. He was so distraught that his sweat became drops of blood falling to the ground. But Jesus' obedience, even to the point of death, was embodied in his words, "My Father, if it be possible, let this cup pass from me; nevertheless, not as I will, but as you will" (Matthew 26:39). Jesus obeyed his Father to the point of death—even death on a cross, which is the most excruciating and torturous method of execution.

Before Jesus' birth, his earthly father, Joseph, faced a dilemma. While engaged to Mary, he learned that she was pregnant. Being a righteous man, he planned to send her away secretly so as not to disgrace her, but an angel told him not to be afraid to take her as his wife, because the child was conceived by the Holy Spirit and would be the Messiah. Without hesitation, Joseph obeyed God and took Mary as his wife, even though he would be shamed by others for marrying a pregnant woman out of wedlock.

Soon after Jesus' birth, Joseph had another dilemma. This time an angel told him to flee and go to Egypt. Joseph and Mary fled with the infant Jesus. Joseph was obedient to God and uprooted his little family twice without understanding the circumstances; once to go to Egypt and then to return home. Without hesitation, he obeyed God and returned to a new home in Nazareth. He had no idea that this would fulfill old prophecies.

Jesus taught about obedience through numerous parables. In the parable of the banquet, he told of a man who prepared a great banquet and invited many guests. He sent out the invitations but many guests delayed. One said that he needed to take care of his oxen; another, that he needed to check on a field he had just bought; still another, that he was distracted with a family issue. The master of the banquet became angry and ordered his servant to invite different guests: the poor, crippled, blind, and lame. This parable illustrated the importance of immediately obeying the Lord when we hear him.

Do not delay when called; go immediately. Obedience is not optional. Those who did not respond immediately faced severe consequences in this parable.

Obedience in the Workplace

To apply this parable, I must promptly obey the Lord and diligently follow him. He may not present another opportunity, and I believe our faith is demonstrated in our response and sense of urgency. Obeying is doing what we are told to do. Employees should obey their employers by doing what they are told just as business leaders and owners have an obligation to obey the Lord.

In his response to the Father, Jesus set the example for obedience. He did what the Father commanded him to do. He obeyed out of love for the Father and in response to the Father's love for him. Jesus said to his disciples in the upper room, "As the Father has loved me, so have I loved you. Abide in my love. If you keep my commandments, you will abide in my love, just as I have kept my Father's commandments and abide in his love" (John 15:9–10). It is simple. If we love Christ, we will obey him, just as he demonstrated his love for the Father through obedience.

If we abide in Christ, we ought to walk in the same way Jesus walked. Our actions express our obedience to Christ's command to love him and others. The interaction between abiding, obeying, and loving Christ is clearly delineated in the apostle John's letter (1 John 2:3–6). We cannot truly walk on a path of righteousness if we do not regularly abide with Christ; it is our only hope of keeping his commandment to love him and to love others.

We love God by obeying his commands (1 John 5:1–4). We must obey even when it is hard and we do not see the outcome. It may cost us much, and we will certainly be pushing up against the world's standards.

Examples of Obedience

As Jesus was teaching the crowds by the Sea of Galilee, he saw two boats, one of which belonged to Simon Peter, who was washing his nets. Jesus asked to borrow the boat to teach the crowds standing on the shore. After Jesus taught, he told Peter to cast his nets into the deep water. Peter replied that they had fished all night and caught nothing, but that he would do as he was told. They caught such a great number of fish that the nets began to tear. Peter signaled for his partners in the other boat to come and help. They filled both boats so full that they began to sink. Peter then fell at Jesus' feet, saying, "Depart from me, for I am a sinful man, O Lord." Jesus replied to Peter, "Don't be afraid; from now on you will be catching men." They returned to shore, and he left everything to follow Jesus (Luke 5:1–11).

I speculate that Peter struggled in his decision to follow Jesus, because leaving everything would have severely hampered the cash flow of his fishing business. Peter was an enigma. Though he dropped his nets full of fish to follow Jesus, he later denied knowing Jesus. After his resurrection, Jesus walked once more with Peter along the Sea of Galilee. In what was their last known conversation, Jesus told Peter to follow him. After three years of being with Jesus, Peter finally understood obedience. From that time on, there was no doubt that he would obey.

I find it interesting how different people responded to Jesus' command to follow him. Zacchaeus immediately came down out of the tree when Jesus asked to come to his home for dinner. He changed from being a tax-collecting extortionist to being a generous man, giving half of his possessions to the poor and repaying those he had cheated. When Jesus called Matthew, another tax collector, he got up immediately and followed. He obeyed despite the probability that he was operating a lucrative business for which he was despised by Jewish society. His immediate obedience was not without consequence. Peter, Zacchaeus, and Matthew were all in.

On the other hand, the rich young ruler did not immediately follow Jesus. We do not know if he ever did, but we know that he had to contemplate a serious request before following Jesus—to sell all he possessed and give it to the poor. What he did not realize was how much more he would gain.

Others also delayed in following Jesus. When a scribe declared that he would follow Jesus wherever he went, Jesus responded, "Foxes have holes, and birds of the air have nests, but the Son of Man has nowhere to lay his head" (Luke 9:58). One disciple wanted to say goodbye to his family first; another wanted to bury his father first. Jesus knew the hearts of all people and that many would want to follow but would be unable to obey because of the sacrifice involved.

Build a Business on a Good Foundation

In the Sermon on the Mount, Jesus' final punch-line business principal was to implement what we hear. Obedience is not just listening but also applying what is understood. To illustrate, Jesus contrasted a foolish man building his house on sand with a wise man building his house on the rock. To only hear Jesus' words is like building a house on the sand, an unstable foundation that gives way, destroying the house. But to hear and apply God's word is like building on a rock foundation that will not give way in the storms of life. Jesus said, "Therefore everyone who hears these words of mine and puts them into practice is like a wise man who built his house on the rock" (Matthew 7:24 NIV).

Build on a good foundation so that when storms come, "the house" you are building will prevail, withstanding the wind and the floods. A good business foundation is built upon obeying God's commands and applying his principles in the marketplace. Being in the architectural profession, we know the importance of building a proper foundation under a structure. On every project, we do extensive research to determine the soil conditions.

Some areas need minimal foundations, while others need piers driven deeply into the bedrock. Without a good foundation, the structure will move, causing cracking and, in some cases, eventual failure.

The same is true for businesses not built on good foundations. Initially, hurriedly building a shallow foundation may seem insignificant because no immediate problems are perceived. It may take several years, but eventually the improperly constructed foundation will move. This movement will cause cracks and sometimes structural compromise. Compromise can then lead to failure. I cannot tell you how many times we have entered existing buildings and noticed that the foundation has allowed the building to shift. The owner always asks if we can fix it. Often, we can offer only cosmetic repairs. Cosmetic repairs may look good for a while, but the problem will always return.

In business, obeying God's commands allows us to build on a good foundation that will stand the test of time. This foundation is needed so that when problems arise, we have the bedrock of deep truth found in God's Word on which to rely. Our well-built house will withstand trials and tribulation (Luke 6:46–49).

As children, we obeyed our parents, or at least we were supposed to. I doubt many of us disobeyed our parents for long. In my family, there was a sure reckoning for my disobedience. Both my dad and stepfather were firm and hard in their discipline. Unlike the political correctness of today, the rod was not spared and my bottom was often red. But that redness was for my eventual good. There is a correlation between obeying my earthly father and obeying my heavenly Father. Disobedience results in discipline, but that discipline is for the purpose of training.

Obedience is a nonnegotiable in the military. If you do not obey, you are either dead or court-martialed. In God's kingdom, we may not see the same severity, but the consequences are much the same. There can be spiritual death and destruction if we do not obey God's commands.

In business, obedience is viewed as a softer command, lacking import. Cheerful obedience to superiors brings unity and peace within a company. The hierarchy of leadership is based upon obedience by subordinates. When our society becomes more autonomous, unwilling to obey authority, then chaos will creep in. Anarchy will result.

The Great Obedience

The night before his crucifixion, Jesus gave the disciples a telling command. He said four times, "If you love me, you will keep my commandments" (John 14:15, 21, 23; 15:10).

The greatest command Jesus gave was to love one another as he has loved us; this love entails laying down our lives for others (John 15:12–13). We must love others, including those hard-to-love family members, employees, and clients. This is an impossible task without the help of the Holy Spirit. Obedience must be exercised just like a muscle if we are ever to be strong in loving others.

Quiet Whispers of the Holy Spirit

Obedience is not something we normally think about in business. Obedience is doing what we hear from the Father through the quiet whispers of the Holy Spirit. Many times, we do not hear his command over a megaphone but rather as a simple prompting inside our hearts. I cannot tell you how many decisions I have made based on this prompting. It is risky; it takes faith, and uncertainty prevails at first. But if it is in God's will, then it becomes evident later; there is always confirmation.

For Further Study

- Matthew 1:18–25; 2:13–15, 19–23: Joseph's example of obedience.
- Matthew 5:19: Obey by practicing and teaching God's commandments to others.
- Matthew 7:24–27: Life of obedience—building on a solid foundation.
- Mark 10:17–22: Story of rich young ruler.
- Luke 5:1–11: The obedience of Peter to follow Jesus.
- Luke 5:10–11; 5:27–28; Matthew 9:9: These left everything to immediately follow Jesus.
- Luke 6:43; 8:15: Bearing fruit comes from obedience.
- Luke 9:23, 57–62: "Follow me," Jesus said.
- Luke 19:1–10: Story of Zacchaeus following Jesus.
- John 5:19: Submit to the authority of the Father.
- John 14:15, 21, 23–24; 15:10: We will obey Jesus' commands if we love him.
- John 14:31: Jesus loved and obeyed the Father.
- John 15:10: If you obey, you are in his love.

16

ACKNOWLEDGING CHRIST

BEING UNASHAMED

One of my greatest struggles in business is being openly unashamed of my faith in front of those who oppose Christianity. It is easy to acknowledge Christ in front of fellow believers, but to be an unashamed witness in front of apathetic or skeptical people is difficult for me. I endeavor to live a somewhat quiet life, allowing my actions to speak louder than my words. But this does not give me a bye in verbally expressing my faith when given the opportunity.

I am not saying that we should browbeat people or wear our religion on our sleeves, but I know there have been good opportunities that I have let slip because of my personal discomfort. This is a shame because of what Jesus said: "And I tell you, everyone who acknowledges me before men, the Son of Man also will acknowledge before the angels of God, but the one who denies me before men will be denied before the angels of God" (Luke 12:8–9).

I am not alone in my struggle either. Even Peter, Jesus' beloved and loyal apostle, did not acknowledge Jesus at times. During their last meal together on the night before Jesus was crucified, Jesus told Peter that he would deny him three times. Peter did not want to believe it. But even before those denials, Peter failed Jesus as he prayed in the garden of Gethsemane; he fell asleep three times although Jesus asked him to stay up and watch with him.

Early the next morning, while Peter waited outside the chief priest's house to learn the verdict of Jesus' trial, he disavowed Jesus three times. When the rooster crowed, Peter remembered Jesus' prediction and left to weep bitterly. Although Peter intimately walked with Jesus during his three-year earthly ministry, at times he struggled with acknowledging him before others.

Nevertheless, we must not forget the redemptive outcome and how greatly God used Peter to build his kingdom. As Jesus also predicted, he built his church upon Peter's faithfulness and determination. Peter acknowledged Jesus and followed him the rest of his life; he even shared his Master's fate of crucifixion. When we are ashamed of Christ and fail to acknowledge him, there is always the hope of redemption for us as well.

I learned from Peter's example that the spirit is willing but the flesh is weak (Matthew 26:41). Yet Christ can make us strong and glorify himself in our lives. That is how we can have the hope of being faithful, just like Peter, and acknowledging Christ in our business dealings.

Our culture changes so rapidly that it makes my head spin. I cannot keep up with current political correctness, but I know that it is increasingly politically incorrect to mention Jesus or God in the public square. The world's system never really has followed God's commands and principles; throughout history, true Christianity has been on trial in every society. Unfortunately, America, a bastion of Christianity since its founding, is following in the steps of other post-Christian cultures, turning its back on the Savior and Lord of the world. But we are not here to win the favor of people. Jesus said we are to acknowledge him before others and not to be ashamed. We must not be fearful to express our convictions in the face of political correctness or hostile, evil people who seek to ruin us.

The same struggle existed in Jesus' day. Many did not profess Jesus out of fear of the Pharisees and the possibility that they would be put out of the synagogue (John 12:42). Being put out of the temple for a Jew meant spiritual and physical disenfranchisement. They would not have access to God and ceremonial sacrifices, and so they would be ostracized by their family and friends, resulting in the loss of relationships, home, and work.

We should never feel the need to apologize for our belief in Jesus. He created everyone and everything. How can we be ashamed of our Creator? He died on a cross so that we may live for all eternity in fellowship with him, the Father, and the Spirit. How can we be ashamed of our Savior?

The truth is that I am proud of my sons. They have accomplished much in their lives, from athletics to academics, and seldom do I fail to acknowledge them. When given the opportunity, I joyfully brag about them and their accomplishments or latest success. Because I love them dearly and am proud of them, I want to promote them and put them in a glorious light.

Likewise, many of our employees have done outstanding

things for the firm. We acknowledge them publicly within our firm and outside as well when given the opportunity. I know how wonderful it feels to be acknowledged and honored when I have done something of which others are proud; I have a sense of appreciation and gratitude. Do you think God may feel the same way when we acknowledge him in front of others? After all, he created us with a nature much like his own.

I should be a good witness through all I do in business. I am asking the Lord to help me be natural yet bold in speaking openly about my faith. I do not want to fear the rejection of people so that I do not share the good news when an opportunity presents itself. There is a fine balance in the business community between minimizing faith in Christ and being self-righteous. Rather than being obnoxiously bold, why not remain humble as one who is offering a real treasure to those who desperately need it?

Our reward in heaven is great when we stand firm and acknowledge Christ before others.

For Further Study

- Matthew 10:32–33; Mark 8:38; Luke 12:8–9: Acknowledge Jesus before others.
- Luke 6:22–23: Our reward is great when we face persecution on account of Christ.
- Luke 8:38–39: Proclaim to others what Jesus has done for you.
- Luke 9:26: Do not be ashamed of or minimize Jesus.
- John 12:42–43: Many did not profess Jesus for fear of being put out of the synagogue.

17

GENEROSITY

POOR WOMAN AND TAX COLLECTORS

G enerosity is a beautifully embedded thread throughout the stories and teachings of the Gospels. No other thread runs so carefully throughout all the parables. Generosity was extended by the very rich and the ultra-poor. It was shown by Zacchaeus, the wealthy tax collector who gave half of his money to the poor, and by the widow who gave her last two coins at the temple. Generosity permeates the Gospels, but not once is it defined by an amount.

Most business leaders disregard generosity in their business dealings out of their own self-interest. Why do we negotiate business from our side of the table and refuse to be generous with other parties? I think it is an issue of self-preservation and the fear of scarcity. We fear there will not be enough for us or that in the future we might be in need. The fear of scarcity drives us to hoard for ourselves and to give minimally to others in need. But generosity is letting go of our fears and trusting God, who is the giver of all wealth.

When I am generous, I bless others. We always desire for others to be generous with us, and we are naturally attracted to those who are generous. Think about when you buy an ice cream cone. When the employee carefully scoops out and measures your scoop to an exact amount, you think to yourself, *Wow, he is being stingy!* But if that same person gives you a large scoop, not measuring but slathering it all over your cup or cone, you think, *Wow, I'll come back here!*

We see the same principle in the baker's dozen. In the old days, a baker always included an extra baked good when filling an order for a dozen. A baker's dozen equals thirteen, which is an extra generous portion. The blessing to the baker is the principle that "with the measure you use, it will be measured to you" (Matthew 7:2; Mark 4:24; Luke 6:38).

Personal Generosity

Business generosity begins with personal generosity. This is developed over time with discipline and practice, eventually becoming a habit in a person's life. Because of our selfish natures, generosity will not come easily; it is not a natural response. Most people I meet have not been born with a generosity gene. It seems to develop as their submission to Christ helps them fight their fear of scarcity. I am convinced that generosity goes to the core of our souls.

Jesus' lifestyle was one of generosity. He best exemplified this through his sacrificial love for us, giving everything for our sakes, including his own life to pay our debt. His generosity and its ramifications affect everything when dealing with others in business.

My personal generosity has had to develop over a lifetime, because I was not naturally generous as a little kid. I remember my dad teaching fairness in a transaction: When I would split a candy bar with my stepsister, he would have one of us divide it and the other choose which piece to take. That developed an exacting science; neither of us wanted to divide it disproportionately and risk ending up with the smaller piece. After all, who would ever give the other person the larger piece and keep the smaller one for himself or herself? Certainly not us as kids. But as I have grown older, this memory drives home the need to show real generosity by becoming that person and offering the bigger piece.

One of the first decisions Marydel and I made as a married couple was to give a large cash wedding gift to our church. The gift was the equivalent of one month's salary for the both of us. Offering this gift was difficult at first for two reasons: to us it was a large sum, and we had no savings at the time. But this set us on a path of being generous as a couple throughout our married life.

Although I have struggled with personal generosity, I have also felt an incredible amount of peace after simple expressions of it. Generosity is like a muscle, growing stronger as it is exercised. Those simple acts of generosity were significant to my heart as I struggled with giving away things that were valuable or meaningful. My heart is still wrapped around earthly possessions at times, and to pry it off is difficult. Once dislodged, however, I rejoice in the overflowing joy that replaces my fear of loss.

For thirteen years, I was a scoutmaster in the Boy Scouts. During my tenure, I had an affection for the ideals and writings of the founder, Lord Baden Powell. As I trained other scoutmasters for numerous years in the original scouting ideals, collecting *Boy Scout Handbooks* became a passion. I subsequently collected all editions of the *Scout Handbook*. Some were very valuable, and one such book, the very first copy, was the envy of all Scout geeks. I purchased it for the outrageous sum of $2,800. After receiving this book, I carefully enshrined it in my bookcase. I was proud as a peacock that I had one of the few prepublished editions of the *Handbook for Boys* by Lord Baden Powell and Ernest Thompson Seton. This was a rare treasure.

After enjoying this book for several years, I decided to give it to my son. I struggled with this decision, as I did not think he would take as much pride in owning it as I had in obtaining it. But I also knew that my heart was wrapped around it. One Christmas, as I placed it in a small case to give to my son, it released in me an immense joy; I was tearing my heart away from my possessions. I next gave an equally important book—a pristine copy of the first edition of the handbook—to my other son. This gift came easier and, though it may sound odd, was my way of giving the larger portion of the candy bar.

Several years ago, I was eating breakfast with a Russian friend who was speaking to audiences in the United States. As we ate, he mentioned that his bag had been lost in Moscow. His companion said that they had purchased a few things at Walmart to tide him over until his bag showed up. Realizing that he had been in the US for three days, I blurted out, "Why don't you come to my house and let me give you some clothes to get you by?"

We drove to my house, and, uncharacteristically, I opened my closet and said, "Take anything you would like." I meant it, but deep inside I hoped he would not take my favorite things. Sure enough, he selected my favorite and most expensive shirts. Oddly enough, it gave me great joy as he took the shirts, several ties (again, my favorites), a sports jacket, and a coat that helped him get through the week.

At one point in my struggle with daily generosity, I decided to give a dollar coin to someone every day for a year. Seeing the joy and surprise on strangers' faces as I handed them a dollar coin was a great blessing to me personally. It only cost me $365.00, but the rewards were well worth it.

While I was speaking at Wheaton College in Illinois, one of the professors on our lecture panel complimented the tie I was wearing. Again, being my favorite—and expensive at $175.00—I gave it to him after the lecture. He was astonished but pleased to have a new tie. I was pleased to get something even better—help in my struggle with possessions. I experienced a deeper joy in giving a favorite thing than I would have had in keeping it. It helped me establish a new and better pattern.

When my children were small, I began putting my change in their piggy banks each night. I continued this discipline as they grew up. We humorously called it the "chunk-change" bank. Twenty years of placing my change in the kids' piggy banks resulted in a handsome sum. That change along with other money we added occasionally paid for several years of their college tuition. For me it was not a big deal, but it was a daily reminder to give to my children. I realized that in God's economy, the important thing is faithfulness. I practice this discipline today for my grandchildren, and the "chunk-change" bank continues to remind me of daily, simple generosity.

Generosity with Employees

Matthew 10:10 says that the laborer deserves his food, or to put it another way, the worker is worth his keep. Often an employee's worth is perceived by how well we pay him or her. We are to pay our employees appropriately (1 Timothy 5:18) and to always extend a hand of generosity, not stinginess.

I have experienced that generosity is best expressed to employees through giving them bonuses. For over thirty years now, our firm has distributed bonuses to the employees; I knew the importance of sharing the profits with those who helped generate them. Employees are not entitled to profits, but I wanted to be a good employer and generously share with them. Since the early days when I had only one employee, I have endeavored to give large bonuses. We have continued to do so every year, and in extremely profitable years, the bonuses swelled proportionately.

One year we received an unexpected million dollars in income. I distributed that to employees, resulting in bonuses that far exceeded some of their salaries. That extreme generosity was not necessarily reciprocated with employee gratitude, yet in my heart I knew that this blessing was prompted by the Holy Spirit. I told them that I did not know what future years held, but while we could, I wanted them to pay off debts and to set their houses in order. After analyzing over thirty-three years of business, I discovered that I had distributed the same percentage of bonuses to my partners and employees as I had received.

Generosity to Partners

I realized that to be a good partner, I had to be generous. I owned the whole company for the first twenty-five years. Ten years ago, I invited two excellent men, Shade O'Quinn and Larry Craighead, to become my partners. They had proven to be great partners by their attitude and work ethic; they took on responsibility far beyond the normal employee and gave their hearts and souls to making the firm successful. I recognized that being a good partner would mean treating them as I wanted to be treated.

As we began the process of our ownership transition, I understood that both new partners were encumbered with debt. When Shade joined the firm, he left his previous practice to serve our large corporate clients. Because of previous nonpaying clients, he was saddled with debt to other consultants. He vowed that he would pay back every cent to his consultants even if it took him the rest of his life. I appreciated his determination to pay what he owed, but I knew for him to be a good partner he would have to enter the ownership transaction without this encumbrance. So for the next year and a half, I gave Shade enough bonus money to pay his consultants and to set him up for success as a partner.

My other partner, Larry, had personal debt that would hamper his ability to focus on buying the company stock. I distributed bonuses to take care of that debt as well. By being generous with my potential partners, I laid a foundation for them to trust me and enabled them to serve our clients without distraction. Later I became the beneficiary of their gratitude and a great partnership.

Ownership Transition Valuation

When we established the value of the firm for ownership transition purposes, I discounted it such that Larry and Shade would purchase stock through an internal company sale. They would be given bonuses based on the proportion of shares they were buying and thus repay me in a promissory note. A CPA and attorney originally valued the firm for more than the sale price. I discounted it to make it affordable for them based on their bonuses in lieu of having to personally borrow additional money. I extended this generosity because that is what I would want someone to do for me. I did not want to enslave them with debt for many years. They reciprocated years later by extending to me bonuses beyond my ownership percentage. The generosity came full circle.

In our recent addition of two younger partners, Shade, Larry, and I continued this generosity. We discounted the price of the shares so that these new owners could also repay with internally generated profits. The firm could have been valued for more based on our previous performance and workload, but again, we discounted it to make it affordable and not encumber these new partners. This is far from the norm of most business transactions and ownership transitions.

In a nonmonetary way, I endeavor to remain generous with my time and expertise to help my new partners become successful in running our business. Even after the sale of my ownership, I have remained with the firm to encourage, mentor, and help bear the burden of the larger issues. Although I do not work on daily architectural problems, I focus my efforts on helping them lead the firm.

Generous but Not Fair

Throughout years of responding to employees' requests, I have stated that I may not always be fair, but I will certainly always be generous. This comes from the parable of the workers in the vineyard. In this parable, Jesus told of a landowner who went out early in the morning to solicit laborers for his field. The first ones he approached agreed on the wage of a denarius for the day's work. As the story continues, the same landowner hired additional workers four more times over the course of the day. He told them that he would pay them "whatever is right" (Matthew 20:4). At the end of the day, he settled accounts with the workers, paying each of them a denarius regardless of the number of hours worked.

In our society, we would call that unfair, but Jesus said this landowner was actually being generous. He paid each of them the wage they had agreed to, but he chose to be more generous with the ones who worked fewer hours. Jesus said, "Are you envious because I am generous?" (Matthew 20:15 NIV). This illustrates the fact that God may not always appear fair, but he is certainly generous.

As I reflected further on the parable, I realized that the master was actually fair to all of his workers. The early laborers became disgruntled because they felt entitled to more than the later hires. Their satisfaction with a denarius turned to bitterness because of what others received. In their eyes, the master was not fair, but he *was* fair in paying the wage to which they had agreed. In the same way, employees must learn to be content with what they have; otherwise, they may become disgruntled, unhappy, and poor performers.

Jesus used this parable to teach not only the generosity required of employers but also the gratitude and contentment expected of employees. Jesus concluded by saying, "So the last will be first, and the first last" (Matthew 20:16). God's kingdom is upside down from the world's viewpoint.

As I have worked with employees, some feel that they should receive the same treatment or the same benefits as all other employees. Equality is fair and appropriate when it comes to employment opportunities and antidiscriminatory practices, but when an employer wants to be generous with one employee while not giving other employees the same treatment, it should not be counted as unfair. When I give an employee a day off to take care of a problem or an illness, it does not mean that everyone else should get that same day off. I can choose to be generous without being obligated to do the same for everyone else. If I were to extend the same generosity to everyone, who would come to work?

Generosity of My Partners

Larry Craighead, my business partner, has expressed generosity to our employees over the last number of years by giving a ham or turkey to all employees at Christmastime. It is always fun seeing him walk in with sixty to seventy boxes to be distributed among the staff. Years ago, we did this as a firm but decided to discontinue the tradition. But because of their big-hearted generosity, Larry and his wife decided to continue the tradition on their own. Employees may never realize the love expressed through this generosity. Though a ham or turkey may not seem like a big deal, it requires considerable care and planning on

Larry's part so our employee family can enjoy a wonderful Christmas meal.

Always Give Away the Best

Though I may have developed a generous nature, I do not always share the best or the biggest. Sometimes I share a book with a colleague or friend. If I have two copies, I give him the one that has a blemish while keeping the best one for myself. The same is true for me in sharing anything; I tend to hold back the best. But I have found that to truly love someone and to be generous, I must give them the best one or the biggest piece—just like with my candy bar.

Spontaneous Generosity

Sometimes it is good to be spontaneously generous. This develops a sense of excitement and fun within a group. There have been many times when I have given a possession to someone who complimented it, as with the tie I mentioned earlier. Since that event with the professor, I have given away many of my ties. I know it is crazy, but it is fun for both me and the recipient.

Our office gathers frequently to celebrate employee anniversaries, birthdays, new births, and the occasional retirement. I find it awkward to stand in front of such a large group of people, but if I can be lighthearted and generous, it makes it a great experience for everyone. We play trivia games about the culture and lore of our firm. At times in the past, I have given cash for correct answers. Other times we have given gift cards to encourage employees in their work efforts. When employees have shown extraordinary effort, we spontaneously reward them with a night out with their spouse or a friend. We have even surprised some outstanding employees with a vacation trip. All these are done spontaneously and in a spirit of fun to encourage our people.

I have also given away knickknacks and furniture to my friends if they liked something in my office. Once my partner Ty commented about the antique podium in my office; it now graces his home entryway. Spontaneously giving helps me develop a discipline and habit of being generous by not holding on to things too tightly.

A View from the Receiver's Side of Things

Some gifts we receive are not necessarily appreciated in the moment, but later on they become precious to us. I tend to become critical if employees or friends do not immediately appreciate what I have given them; shame on me. Especially as I have noticed in my own life that things I have received became more meaningful over time. Years ago, my mom gave me an expensive and beautiful world globe. I was casually appreciative at the time, but its value has increased in my heart as my mother has grown older. It has now become one of my most precious possessions.

I have learned not to judge if immediate gratitude is not expressed by the recipient. Sometimes thoughtful contemplation is required to appreciate what they have received. My responsibility is to be generous, not to expect gratitude.

Christ was generous and did not require gratitude in exchange. He freely gave, although many did not realize the gift's value until later. Our journey of faith may require time for us to become grateful for what we receive. Our responsibility is to give with open hands and without expectations.

Give in secrecy, not drawing credit to yourself. If you are to honor God, the giver of all wealth, allow him to receive all the glory. When you are generous, do so quietly and not for notoriety or credit. Our generosity is a form of worship to the one who has been generous to all.

Biblical Examples of Extravagant Generosity

There are several examples of extravagant generosity in the Gospels, but none as great as the anointing of Jesus with the alabaster jar of expensive perfume. In all four Gospel accounts, the woman who anointed Jesus used perfume costing a year's wage, probably around twenty thousand dollars in current value. In one account, the woman broke the flask as a sign of true honor so it could not be used again. She poured the perfume over Jesus' head while he reclined at dinner, anointing him and his body before his death and burial. She may not have realized the significance of what she was doing at the time, but this extreme generosity was an act of worship.

In the same spirit of humble generosity, a poor widow went to the temple and placed an offering of two small copper coins in the temple treasury. Jesus immortalized this woman in Scripture by saying that she gave more than all the others, because she gave all she possessed. No one could have given more for the kingdom than this poor widow gave that day. Jesus commended her for her generosity, not because of the amount but because she gave more than all the rich who had put in large sums of money. In fact, the widow's two coins were less than one percent of a day's wage, about sixty-three cents today, but they were all she had to live on. Is it not interesting that this is what Jesus requested of the rich young ruler—to give it all? Jesus had a flair for striking at the heart.

The Gospels offer these women as examples to illustrate the principles of stewardship and sacrificial generosity. Do you have the courage to follow in their footsteps?

For Further Study

- Proverbs 11:24–26: A generous person.
- Psalm 112:5–9: A generous person.
- Matthew 6:3–4: Generosity and giving done in secret.
- Matthew 7:2; Mark 4:24; Luke 6:38: The measure you use will be measured to you.
- Matthew 10:10; Luke 10:7: Laborers deserve their wages.
- Matthew 20:1–16: Parable of the laborers in the vineyard.
- Matthew 26:6–13: Woman pouring ointment on Jesus.
- Mark 12:41–44; Luke 21:1–4: Poor widow at the temple.
- Mark 14:3–9; Luke 7:36–50; John 12:1–8: Anointing of Jesus.

18

PRAYING, RETREATING, AND ABIDING

MOUNTAINTOP EXPERIENCES

For any engine to work properly, it must be fueled. As businessmen and businesswomen in God's economy, we are called by God to be economic engines for his kingdom. The fuel to power our engines is abiding prayer with God, and the best way to do that is through retreats and being alone with him.

Jesus spent much time in prayer, often spending all night abiding with the Father. Jesus continually withdrew to desolate places to pray early in the morning and to have fellowship with his Father. His retreats were frequently to high places, up on a mountain or to the temple in Jerusalem, which was the highest point in the city.

Before selecting the twelve apostles, Jesus went to a mountain and spent all night in prayer with God; in the morning, he appointed the twelve. After performing great miracles, Jesus would withdraw from the crowds to a lonely place to pray. He also retreated with his disciples upon their return from being sent out on mission; those retreats rested and empowered them to perform more miracles.

In John, prior to the miracle of the feeding of the five thousand, Jesus took his men up on the mountain. And immediately following, after he dismissed the crowds, he returned to the mountainside to pray. This repeated pattern of withdrawing to pray before and after accomplishing great things was an important aspect of abiding with his Father, setting the example for us to follow. Personally, I find it impossible to understand God's will for my business unless I abide and quietly seek his counsel.

Many years ago, I took my key leaders on a retreat to Santa Fe, New Mexico, to make imperative decisions for the firm. Away from the noise of the office, we were able to discuss and make decisions that have served us well for the past fifteen years. In fact, I am certain that some of those decisions will benefit the firm for the entirety of its existence. We had such a meaningful time during that retreat that we have continued to schedule annual retreats for the leaders and owners to get away together. Retreating is crucial if we are to work together as a company to accomplish our goals.

During the most heart-wrenching night of his earthly life, Jesus retreated to the Father in the garden of Gethsemane the night before his crucifixion. His sweat became like drops of blood as he prayed to escape the inevitable events of the next day. He yielded to God's will, regardless of his desire to avoid this excruciating death. Likewise, we may cry out to God with our desires, but we should always ask God for his will to be done in us. This will guarantee successful answers to our prayers.

We are always to pray and not lose heart. Being persistent in our prayers will affect God, as is demonstrated in the parable of the persistent widow. In Luke's account, a widow kept pleading with a judge for justice. Finally, the judge granted her request just to get rid of her. It pleases God when we earnestly and continually come to him, beseeching him for our requests. Our persistence demonstrates our faith. He will give expediently, because he said, "And will not God bring about justice for his chosen ones, who cry to him day and night?" (Luke 18:7 NIV).

In another parable, a man was in bed when a neighbor came knocking at midnight to request bread for a visiting friend. Jesus used this parable to illustrate audacious prayer, because the man kept knocking until he received what he asked for. We should not ask God casually but with full expectation that he will answer like a good father. These parables are an admonition to ask God with persistence and audacity.

Desperate Prayer

I have often cried out to God when I desperately needed help in my architectural practice. One such instance was when we were served a notice of a lawsuit. A year prior to receiving this notice, a roof on one of our projects had collapsed during a torrential rainstorm. Although the collapse was not our fault, we were still trapped in a lawsuit and felt helpless. I beseeched the Lord, crying out to him for wisdom on how to approach this situation. The next year the problem was resolved. As I prayed time and again, God gave me wisdom, insight, and skill to negotiate an equitable settlement with all parties. I prayed persistently like the widow before the unjust judge, knowing that God would protect us regardless of the outcome of the lawsuit.

Frequently, when we pray with desperation, it is because we want to get out of a situation or we want something to go well. Jesus prayed differently on his last night. He prayed for the Father's will, not his own, to be done (Luke 22:42). When beseeching the Lord, know that he is a good Father who gives good gifts to his children. Remember that because God loves us, he wants the best for us. Jesus told us to ask and it will be given, seek and we will find, knock and the door will be opened (Luke 11:9). So in everything we do, we must remember the good things the heavenly Father will give if we simply ask him.

The Lord's Prayer

The Lord's Prayer is the perfect example of praying simply for our needs. Jesus taught us to pray using this prayer. It is simple enough for a child to understand and complete enough to satisfy the most learned theologian. If only I would employ my childlike faith and believe in the adequacy of this prayer for my complicated life.

Abiding in Christ Results in Bearing Fruit

As we have seen, Jesus retreated to high places to abide with the Father. Abiding means dwelling with, and dwelling requires time; abiding also means obedient surrender. Jesus spent vast amounts of time with his heavenly Father, resulting in the ultimate bond between them. We have difficulty understanding this bond, much like comprehending the Trinity, but we too can have a similar bond with Jesus if we abide with him.

John 15 explains the importance of abiding in Jesus. He says that we can do nothing apart from him, just as branches are unable to bear fruit or survive apart from abiding in the vine.

The simple lessons I learned from the vine described in John 15:1–8 are:

1. Every branch that does not bear fruit is removed.
2. Branches are pruned to bear better fruit.
3. If we do not abide in Christ, then we cannot bear fruit.
4. God is glorified when we bear much fruit.
5. We abide in Christ by obeying his commands.
6. By abiding in Christ, we will have full joy in our lives.

If you ask in faith, you will receive the request. As Jesus instructed his disciples the morning they walked by the withered fig tree, if you have faith and do not doubt, you can do miraculous things: "Therefore I tell you, whatever you ask in prayer, believe that you have received it, and it will be yours" (Mark 11:24). Jesus also said that "if two of you on earth agree about anything they ask, it will be done for them by my Father in heaven" (Matthew 18:19). Though these seem like simple, formulaic approaches to prayer, we must understand that Jesus' emphasis was on asking in faith.

Keeping God's commands is an indication of truly abiding in him. Jesus told his disciples, "If anyone loves me, he will keep my word, and my Father will love him, and we will come to him and make our home with him" (John 14:23). The more intimately we know Christ, the more likely we are to obey his commands. Our redeemed nature yearns to follow Christ's commands, because we want to be pleasing to him.

For Further Study

- Matthew 6:9–13: The Lord's Prayer—simple and perfect for our soul.
- Matthew 7:7–11: Ask the Lord who responds as a good father, desiring to give good gifts.
- Matthew 14:13, 23; Mark 1:35; 6:46; Luke 4:42; 5:16; 6:12: Jesus withdrew and prayed.
- Matthew 18:19–20: If two or three agree on anything, there is answered prayer.
- Matthew 21:22; Mark 11:24: Ask in faith by prayer.
- Matthew 26:39: Jesus praying in the garden of Gethsemane.
- Mark 3:7; 6:30–32; Luke 9:10: Jesus took his disciples to retreat.
- Luke 4:42; 5:16: Jesus went to a desolate place.
- Luke 6:12: Jesus prayed all night.
- Luke 11:5–10: Persistent and audacious prayer—story of the midnight bread.
- Luke 11:11–13: God as the good Father.
- Luke 18:1: Always pray and never give up.
- Luke 18:1–8: Parable of the persistent widow.
- John 14:13–14: Ask the Lord for anything to glorify the Father.
- John 15:1–8: Abiding with Jesus results in bearing fruit.

19

SHREWDNESS

OFFICE LEASES AND BUYING HOUSES

L ooking back on my business career, one of the shrewdest
moves I made was in negotiating the lease of my office. In
1988, I moved into an eighty-year-old warehouse that had been
restored and converted into an office building. It was in the old
warehouse district of downtown Dallas where few businesses
were located at the time. I took a risk and asked the owner of the
building if I could negotiate a lease. He was thrilled, because I
would be the first tenant in this five-story building.

I requested a low monthly payment, and I was willing to be
creative to achieve that goal. I also wanted to know the extent of
my liabilities for utilities, operations, and maintenance. Today
this is called a triple-net lease. The landlord was eager to have
me as the first tenant, and I was eager to be in there because it
was such a cool old building.

So we negotiated a lease that capped my financial exposure.
I reasoned that profitability during my first year of occupancy

did not guarantee I would be as profitable at the end of the lease in three years. I therefore negotiated a higher monthly payment in the first year with decreasing payments over the subsequent years. In other words, the first year's payments were more than the third year's payments. I knew that if I were in business now, I would probably be in business later, but by paying more now, I was assured to have less overhead in the future.

We have continued this practice over the past twenty-five years of lease negotiations, which is counter to the normal real-estate pattern of increasing monthly payments over the term of a lease. This was a shrewd move on our part, because we could control expenses and know our maximum financial exposure for the future.

We also capped lease expenses by not requiring an expensive "finish-out" of our office space. We have an open-plan office environment that keeps our overhead costs low because of the minimal construction costs. Our offices are sparsely finished but nicely adorned. In fact, every first-time visitor to our office comments about our wonderful space in this fantastic historic building.

Our actual effective lease rate has not increased over the past twenty-five years. I know of no others who have accomplished this. We negotiated what was critical to us and gave concessions on the owner's principal issues. Therefore, we constructed our finish-out once, became good compliant tenants, and did not require high maintenance. Our landlords always seem to like us.

The Shrewd Manager

One of the potentially confusing parables in the Gospels is the parable of the shrewd, dishonest manager. A good friend who serves as a missionary could not understand why Jesus would commend a dishonest manager. I can understand his point. However, as I meditated on this parable, I realized that what Jesus commended was the shrewdness with which the manager navigated his dire circumstances, not his dishonesty.

In Luke 16, Jesus told his disciples about a manager accused of wasting his master's possessions. The rich man called the manager to give an account of what he had managed. As he realized that he was losing his job, the manager went to his master's debtors (vendors and suppliers in today's vernacular) to renegotiate their contracts. He told each to cut their bill by a certain percentage to their benefit. In return, he expected them to treat him favorably when he was out of his job.

Jesus concluded with the master's commending the dishonest manager for his shrewdness. Jesus went on to explain that we should use worldly wealth to gain friends for ourselves so that when it is gone, we may be welcomed. Jesus commended the shrewd manager for making friends and using wealth for that purpose. In the parable, three things happened:

1. The shrewd manager prepared for his departure so that he would be received by his previous "vendors." He gave advantage to them by reducing their debts, which was in their best interest.
2. The master commended the manager for his preparation and shrewdness.
3. The shrewd manager made friends using his master's wealth.

The reason I like this parable is that it commends creative thinking and shrewdness in navigating the world. There is nothing wrong with developing friendships using the leverage of money. Many leaders of ministries and nonprofits develop friendships with those who fund them.

Jesus said that the children of this world are shrewder than the children of the light. He does not suggest that we embrace the world's value system but that we be shrewd in our dealings with those in the world. Shrewdness is better in dealing with people than naivety or lack of creativity.

In another instance, Jesus commanded his disciples to be as shrewd as serpents and as innocent as doves (Matthew 10:16 NIV). He instructed his disciples to be shrewd in dealing with the world prior to sending them on a mission. He told them to be on their guard because they would be hated, afflicted, and discriminated against while sharing the gospel.

Christians today may not commend shrewdness as a virtue, thinking it taboo or inappropriate and a bad characteristic to possess. But I have asked God to give me shrewdness in all my business dealings.

Shrewdness is most effective when dealing with corporate business or government entities while navigating through the world's standards. I do not think many people want to pay the maximum suggested by the IRS, and it is widely accepted as foolish to give more information than is required in an IRS audit. That is where shrewdness comes in. We want to be shrewd in how we deal with the government, not doing anything illegal or unethical but certainly not being naïve.

We must be careful when using shrewdness for our own benefit so it does not become a detriment to others. When dealing with individuals, I find that shrewdness may be appropriate if carefully used, but I always pursue the other person's best interest and do not put him or her at a disadvantage.

Practical Applications

One of the shrewd things I do in business is understand my clients' needs so I can better serve them. If I do what they ask without understanding the required needs, we might get our clients and ourselves in trouble as professionals. Our clients have hired us as specialists, and therefore we must be expert enough to understand the problem and give them the correct solution. Shrewdness aids us in delivering what our clients need in a way that is inoffensive and appreciated rather than appearing combative.

Years ago, the IRS Tax Code allowed a write-off up to fifty dollars without requiring a receipt for each business expense. I applied this regulation to my travel. Every time I traveled, I would expense fifty dollars to the travel budget using this allowance. Over the years, I wrote off many business travel expenses for legitimate trips because of this IRS allowance. I therefore did not need to keep many travel receipts. I could expense travel costs and save our company money in taxes because of this allowance.

Many folks are not inclined to write down their mileage when they go on an errand or drive for business purposes. I kept a log in my car documenting every time I drove my car for business. This added up. I think it shrewd to write down your mileage when using your car for business and thus take advantage of the IRS-approved expense allowance. Over many years, this proved to be great tax savings for our company.

I also use credit cards that accumulate miles on different airlines. Gaining air miles on business expenses with no extra effort is wonderful. I use accumulated miles on ministry trips and save a lot of money, especially since I cannot write off personal ministry expenses. By taking advantage of such opportunities, we can reap benefits that may otherwise be lost.

Shrewdness is a close cousin to creativity. I find that being creative in business dealings allows me to be a shrewd businessman. Thinking outside the box by creatively approaching problems allows me to cut our business expenses without knowingly using shrewdness in any unethical or illegal way. Shrewdness can be used to accomplish great things for legitimate business and God's kingdom.

When I purchased our last house, I negotiated our real-estate contract. I knew that the owner did not want a lot of hassle in selling his home. I also observed that he was thrifty, not using a realtor to avoid their fees. I tried to determine what he really needed out of the real-estate transaction and, at the same time, achieve my goal of a lower price. I approached him with the idea of providing a hassle-free transaction by not requiring inspections and accepting the house as is, by closing the transaction promptly, and by offering a large earnest money deposit. He allowed me to pay a reduced price because I enabled him to avoid hassles and save money on inspection and repair costs.

In the real-estate transaction for our vacation home, the owner wanted to sell quickly. The house had been on the market for over a year, and he was tired. Again, I approached the seller with the idea of buying the house quickly and without hassles. I would accept the house as is, close quickly, put up a large earnest money contract, and even buy some of his furniture. That would save him from moving the furnishings that he did not want. He accepted a reduced house price knowing that this transaction would be executed quickly and he would receive much-needed money since the home had been on the market for a lengthy time.

Several years ago, we were served papers for a lawsuit on a project. Although we were not at fault, we quickly settled with our client and their insurance company. It was a shrewd move for us because, even though a lengthy trial and legal expenses would have proved our innocence, they could equally damage our relationship with the client. We also estimated that trial expenses would cost us more than our settlement. As a result, our client was appreciative of the reduced hassles and our willingness to mitigate their loss, although we were not legally obligated to. Our goodwill has been rewarded by our client giving us future work.

My use of shrewdness means looking at things from a unique perspective and employing creativity that benefits us and those we serve. It results in a win for everyone and continues to enforce the Golden Rule of "doing for others as we wish they would do for us."

For Further Study

- Luke 16:1–9: The story of the dishonest but shrewd manager.

20

PREPARATION AND PLANNING

READY FOR ACTION

In 2016, cold water was thrown into our faces. Russian hackers hit our firm with a ransomware virus, holding us hostage by locking down some of our computer servers. We immediately shut down as many computers as possible to stop the virus from spreading, isolating it before it destroyed our network. Some damage was done, but if we had not prepared for such a virus, we might be out of business today.

Through prior preparation, we had backed up our computer network system offsite so that in a catastrophe we could reinstall our precious information. We have done thousands of projects for our clients, and this information is critical for our existence. All our drawings are done by computer software, and massive files must be stored for retrieval. We constantly access these files to do our work.

This incident drove home the importance of taking seriously the Boy Scouts of America's motto, "Be prepared." It had been drilled into me not only as a Scout in my youth, but also as a scoutmaster. I thank God our firm was prepared in this instance.

Jesus devoted his last days to admonishing the disciples to prepare for the future. The most important preparation for all humanity is to have salvation in Jesus Christ. If we are not prepared before we die, then it will be too late. Our eternity is set; there is no going back.

Jesus told several parables about being prepared. The best known is the parable of the ten virgins who were awaiting the bridegroom for the wedding ceremony. Five of the virgins had wisely prepared ahead of time; they not only had oil in their lamps but also extra oil in case their lamps ran out. The other five virgins were considered foolish because they did not bring extra oil.

The bridegroom was delayed, and the ten virgins' lamps went out. With their extra oil, the wise virgins continued burning their lamps, but the foolish virgins had to leave to buy extra oil. Unfortunately for them, while they were gone, the bridegroom arrived, taking the prepared virgins to the wedding banquet. Then the door was shut. This illustrates the importance of always being prepared. Preparation means taking care of things ahead of time to be ready for a potential event.

Preparing for the Unexpected

We never know when a lawsuit might come upon us. Over the past thirty-five years, our firm has produced thousands of projects for clients. Every once in a great while, a letter will arrive on our doorstep naming us in a lawsuit by someone who has allegedly been hurt in one of our projects. In our industry, these are known as "slip and falls" and are often handled by unscrupulous lawyers. As of this writing, we have not had to pay any plaintiffs for "slip and fall" injuries; nor has our firm been sued for incompetency errors in our professional documents or service. Although we have been in several lawsuits, we are prepared to defend ourselves and have avoided any judgments because of the quality of our documents and services.

We endeavor to provide carefully executed construction drawings, ensuring that all building codes and safety factors are considered. We double-check our drawings before issuing them for the contractor to build, and most of the time we inspect our jobs to ensure that the construction complies with our drawings. Through our careful preparation, we can defend ourselves and avoid lawsuit settlements.

Every business must be prepared for the financial times ahead. Our firm has not incurred debt in its operations. This allows us to be well prepared in the event of an economic downturn or a catastrophic financial event. When the 9/11 collapse of the Twin Towers happened, we were prepared. Right after that event, many banks closed briefly and business as usual was altered for the better part of that week. Although we never anticipated a terrorist attack, we were prepared with cash on hand and could open our doors the next day, allowing our employees to endure this tragedy with confidence.

Having financial margin is critical in preparing for the uncertain days ahead. This margin includes not having financial encumbrances and debt obligations that restrict you from operating during dire circumstances. Liquidity is also imperative to having financial margin. We carefully set aside profit in our company so that we may have immediate liquidity margin for any unforeseen event.

Ready for Action

Wise businesspeople plan for the future. They not only plan for worst-case scenarios but also have backup plans. When I was a scoutmaster, we would have a backup plan for our events. If a campout had unusual rain, we had planned an alternative location and event. There should always be a plan B in case plan A fails.

Although we cannot see into the future or have guarantees, we can be prepared, as Jesus illustrated in his parables. As mentioned earlier in the parable of the ten bridesmaids, the five wise virgins took additional oil even though they did not see an immediate need for it. They also worked together as a team, looked ahead, and had margin in their lives, exemplified by taking the extra flask of oil. They thought through what they might need and did not go hastily. They did not risk losing their opportunity by becoming codependent with the unprepared; instead, they suggested a responsible remedy. They remained effective, because had they shared their oil, all ten would have failed. By not being prepared, the five foolish virgins missed their opportunity.

Preparing for what is not in our control is critical if we are to be able to execute the duties required of us. We must think ahead and have backup plans for everything. The military excels at this because the stakes are high. They even execute war games so that they may prepare for any event that might unfold. Planning is not only wise but is also a demonstration of faith because we are not leaving things to chance. We are faithfully preparing ourselves for the future as Jesus exhorted. We are never guaranteed what will happen in the future, but we can plan to the best of our abilities to deal with any scenario when it does materialize.

Because we do not know when Christ will return, we need to prepare now. God's kingdom is for those who have prepared, just like the five bridesmaids. We must remember that our business is a training ground for eternity if we are to operate in God's kingdom. This preparation means doing what is necessary for the future when we do not see it. Everything we do in our business should be with a view toward eternity. We must prioritize the important and not be distracted with the unimportant. This requires discipline.

We are admonished to "be dressed ready for service and keep [our] lamps burning" (Luke 12:35 NIV). Since the inception of my firm, I have kept this exhortation in mind. I have been ready for service and to be deployed at any time. I did not take on debt in my career, and I do not have restrictions that keep me from making necessary adjustments if I am called by God to do something differently. I carry a light backpack by not having encumbrances that would keep me from being flexible and available to serve in any way God might require.

I endeavored to prepare my partners for our firm's leadership transition by spending precious time with them in mentorship and coworking in everyday business situations. In two different sales, I released my leadership of the firm. These sales allowed the firm to continue under great leadership and to not be restricted by me. They also enabled me to deploy my proceeds from the sale as the Lord directed into his kingdom work of taking care of the poor.

We should always have an attitude of watchfulness like the

servant who watched for his master to return from a wedding banquet so he could immediately open the door for him. It was good for that servant when the master found him watching and waiting. Jesus will return at an hour when we do not expect him, so we must be prepared, watching and waiting.

For Further Study

- Matthew 25:1–13: Parable of the ten virgins with lamps.
- Luke 12:35–40: Watchful servant and ready for service.

21

UNITY

KINGDOM DIVIDED

For a business to operate successfully, there must be unity within its ranks. A house divided falls. A kingdom divided is ruined. It is my conviction that leadership must be united on most critical issues. This does not mean we cannot have disagreements, but we must be unified in the outcome. We must conclude with working in the same direction. Luke 11:17 (NIV) says, "Jesus knew their thoughts and said to them: 'Any kingdom divided against itself will be ruined, and a house divided against itself will fall.'"

Nothing has been more important in my business partnership than being unified. My partners and I share the value of having unity as we work together. We do not agree on every issue, but we support one another in the decision we collectively make. Our pursuit of unity has blessed me greatly. As issues arise, we carefully vet them among ourselves; we respect and listen to each other. We might disagree on certain issues, but before we exit the subject, we agree on a solution and then support one another in the follow-through.

I do not always get my way, which can be frustrating, but I place myself in the hands of my partners because I value unity. Nothing affects employees as much as unity among the partnership and ownership of a company. It is just like unity among parents when we are growing up. If our parents always fought and lacked unity, we became insecure as children. The same insecurity results when a company's leadership openly disagrees and displays disunity.

When our firm has a management meeting with managers, associates, and principals, we discuss difficult topics, including employees' performances, clients' issues, and opportunities to serve them. In a room of twenty men and women, there will not always be agreement. But before we leave, we pursue unity as a team. In my years of running our company, we have not had outbreaks of anger or severe disagreements. We come into the meeting with a spirit of unity, knowing that we can speak our piece and tell the truth. It is safe, because we have developed a culture of unity.

When someone has seriously offended (sinned against) us, we have a biblical pattern for responding in a way that has the best chance of preserving unity. First, we quietly confront the person who has hurt us. The hope is that we can resolve the issue, preserve the offender's dignity, and heal the damaged relationship. If this ends in a stalemate, we need to go to the second step: bring a respected third party to offer an objective perspective and help us settle the matter. If that fails, and only as a last resort, we take it to the appropriate authority. Because the goal is always redemption and restored fellowship—not punishment—every step should be conducted carefully and prayerfully. This is the best way to resolve a conflict or to confront someone we believe has wronged us. If our hearts desire restoration and we follow this pattern, we promote a culture of unity.

For Further Study

- Matthew 12:25: A house divided will not stand.
- Matthew 12:30: If you do not gather, you scatter.
- Matthew 18:15–17: Confronting when wronged.
- Mark 3:24–25; Luke 11:17: A kingdom divided cannot stand.

22

FORGIVENESS AND MERCY

SECOND CHANCES

As I thought through my experiences in running a successful business, being merciful or forgiving did not immediately come to mind. I do not think I have intentionally forgiven or consciously been merciful very often. However, Jesus taught that forgiveness is crucial in our relationships.

I can remember instances when I needed to forgive someone and when I needed to be forgiven for some of the bonehead things I have done. My nature is to want to be forgiven far more than to go through the difficult process of forgiving others. I want my actions to be redeemed, but I am slow to forgive others' sinful actions.

The morning after Jesus cursed a fig tree, his disciples noticed that the tree had withered. They were amazed and asked Jesus more about this phenomenon. Jesus explained to them about the importance of faith as well as the necessity to forgive others when praying if they desire the Father to answer. He warned that if they would not forgive others, the Father would not forgive them; and when their sin hindered their fellowship with God, they should not expect God to answer their prayers. If we desire for God to answer our prayers, then we must place our faith in him and have a heart that has forgiven others.

Daily Conduits of Forgiveness

My business partners and I practice open communication, giving us the freedom to express concerns and to come to one another when offended. The door swings both ways when we need to ask each other for forgiveness. This openness and vulnerability that I have learned with my partners has helped me keep short accounts. We do not allow resentments, frustrations, and divisions to creep in, because we want to be a conduit of forgiveness to each other. There have been times when my partner Shade O'Quinn has said something that offended me, and I have reacted in a less-than-gracious way. Later, when he came to ask if he had offended me, we were given the opportunity to practice mutual forgiveness. It is a beautiful relationship, helping us to be better partners to one another.

When Jesus taught his disciples how to pray, he told them to ask not only for daily bread but also for daily forgiveness. We may expect to receive this forgiveness if we forgive others who sin against us. We must be daily conduits of forgiveness, forgiving those who offend us. The mercy and forgiveness found in the Lord's Prayer is a directive to not hold grudges or allow resentment and bitterness to creep into our hearts.

Temptations to sin will come. In Luke 17:1–4, we are told that if a brother sins against us, we are to rebuke him, and if he repents, we are to forgive him. We are to do this even if he sins against us numerous times. This means I should be generous in my forgiveness, even in numerous conflicts, so long as there is genuine repentance. Some of these conflicts may be over the same issue, but I am always called to forgive. This does not, however, give us a license to sin against one another.

Forgive Your Brother

In Matthew 18:15, Jesus said if a brother sins against you, then you are to go and show him his fault. This is a famous passage where Jesus explains church discipline. If the reader continues past this short section, Peter asks the question that we all wonder, " 'How often will my bother sin against me, and I forgive him? As many as seven times?' Jesus said to him, 'I do not say to you seven times, but seventy-seven times'" (Matthew 18:21–22).

Then Jesus tells the parable of the unmerciful servant. A servant owed his master an exorbitant amount of money. Unable to pay, he asked for mercy, and the gracious master forgave his debt. Later, this servant found a fellow servant who owed him a small amount of money. The servant did not forgive his fellow servant but began to choke him and demand the money; when the fellow servant begged for patience to pay it back, the servant refused and had him thrown into prison until the debt was paid. Jesus used this example to show that just as God forgives our massive debt of sin, so we must forgive others.

So many times we refuse to extend mercy while demanding it for ourselves. It is easier to ask for mercy and forgiveness than it is to extend it to those who have sinned against us.

In this parable, the master had loaned the unmerciful servant ten thousand talents. A talent in those days was worth about twenty years of a laborer's wage; this really was an incredible amount of money. Yet the amount of money owed to the servant was about four months of a laborer's wage, which was minor in comparison. The servant was unmerciful to those who owed him money, even after asking and receiving mercy from his master. When the master learned of what had transpired, he handed the unmerciful servant over to the jailers to be tortured until the debt was repaid. We must learn that there are severe consequences if we do not forgive from our hearts, as Jesus commanded us to do.

But please understand that forgiveness does not equate to reconciliation. Unlike God's forgiveness that imputes righteousness, our forgiveness does not. For a relationship to be restored, the offender must be truly repentant of his or her sin against us.

Forgive Those Who Sin against Us

Our firm has been stiffed by several unscrupulous developers in the past. In the beginning years of our firm, we provided architectural services to developers of assisted living centers and senior housing. During that time, many developers were entering this real-estate market hoping to make quick money. As with any get-rich-quick scheme, shortcuts were taken and paying the architects was a low priority for these undercapitalized developers.

We provided architectural planning services for a Florida developer entering the elderly housing market. As we proceeded with the work, we sent invoices that went unpaid. After several months of work, I confronted the developer, saying that we could not continue working until we received payment for services rendered. In a brash and ugly way, he told us to keep working and not worry about getting paid. We refused, and he refused to pay our fee. Such confrontations are unpleasant and frustrating. An out-of-state client is difficult to collect from legally. I therefore forgave his debt, but I also had to forgive him for lying and stealing from me. Once I did this, I experienced peace even though I had lost a significant amount of money.

Another such instance occurred with a developer from Beaumont, Texas. I was suspicious at our initial meeting but, desiring to be a good servant and provide quality service, I did preliminary work and then sent him an invoice. Like the Floridian, he refused to pay until I did further work. We all know where that ends up. He was later arrested, tried, and convicted for being an accessory to murder, proving he was an evil man. Although he had taken advantage of me as a young architect, I forgave his debt and his treatment of me in business.

On a California project, we were providing services to a large national commercial client. As our consultant, we employed a mechanical engineer the client had demanded we use. Our normal practice is to select our own consultants from among people we feel are competent and with whom we have history. But to comply with our client, we elected to use their suggested mechanical engineer. As time would prove, the engineer was not careful and made a severe mistake on the project. His carelessness resulted in a large change order. Our client demanded that we remedy the problem and pay for the mistake.

The client knew that we hired this consultant based on their demands, but they were holding us accountable for his mistake. We paid $135,000 to correct the problem; the consulting engineer ran and hid. He would not return phone calls or respond to correspondence or even legal demands. Being an out-of-state engineer from the Northeast working on a project in California made it even more complicated. Finally, we had to forgive his debt, after having paid the client for the damages. In my heart, I also had to forgive this engineer for what he had done to us by refusing to talk or take ownership of his responsibilities. The sad thing is that the client never gave us credit for paying for the engineer's mistakes. Forgiveness also resolved my heart's attitude toward the client.

Mercy on Enemies

Jesus taught that we should love our enemies: "But love your enemies, and do good, and lend, expecting nothing in return, and your reward will be great, and you will be sons of the Most High, for he is kind to the ungrateful and the evil. Be merciful, even as your Father is merciful" (Luke 6:35–36).

In order to love, we must forgive our adversaries and have mercy on them. Holding something against an enemy makes it impossible to love him or her. Without forgiveness and mercy, we cannot begin the process of loving.

Second Chances

Just as the Golden Rule says to do for others as we wish that they would do for us, we should have mercy on each other. Jesus' greatest act of mercy was inviting and enabling us to live with him in his kingdom through his substitutionary death. We could never justify ourselves or be good enough. It is truly mercy that has saved us from our sin.

I love the part of the story in Mark 10:21 when Jesus looked at the rich young ruler and loved him. This rich young ruler knelt before Jesus, earnestly seeking eternal life. He asked, "What must I do?" Mark records that Jesus loved him. In their interaction, Jesus had mercy and understanding of this man's condition. God's mercy is for those who fear him.

I love second chances. Mercy and forgiveness are demonstrated by giving someone a second chance. Jesus told a parable of a man who had a fig tree growing in his vineyard; when he looked for fruit on it and found none, he said, "For three years now I've been coming to look for fruit on this fig tree and haven't found any. Cut it down! Why should it use up the soil?" (Luke 13:7 NIV). But the caretaker of the vineyard said, "Leave it alone for one more year, and I'll dig around it and fertilize it. If it bears fruit next year, fine! If not, then cut it down" (Luke 13:8–9 NIV). This is a good example of extending mercy by giving second chances, an example that we ought to follow, especially with employees.

Remember my two movie business partners and the investment terms we agreed on in chapter three? Even though the terms were far more generous to them than their initial proposal, they were eventually unable to meet the obligations of our agreement. I was disappointed, of course, when the five-year term concluded and the loan could not be repaid. We met, along with my attorney, to discuss how to deal with our problem. I had a difficult decision to make: Should I exercise my legal right for nonperformance and force a judgment on them?

Such decisions are not easy. Caught in the tension between

my rights and my desire to live by a higher standard, I carefully weighed the options. I believed in God's ability to see *me* through regardless of the financial outcome of this deal. More importantly, I believed in the brothers, their mission, and their potential to see it through.

We negotiated another five-year loan with similar terms as the original. During this time, they released two films with Sony Pictures. We released a fourth film, this time through Lions Gate Entertainment, which has now become a blockbuster success at the box office. Now as chairman of the board and 25 percent owner of their production company, I am encouraged to see how God is rewarding this extension of mercy.

There is a difference between mercy and forgiveness. Mercy allows the chance of renegotiation and future opportunity. Mercy is extended out of a love and compassion for the person. I care deeply for these partners, and although their payments were due, extending an opportunity to rework the terms showed mercy.

I've also invested in other young entrepreneurs who have been unable to make payments on promissory notes. As a lender, I always realize the risk associated with new business startups. The future is hard to predict, and circumstances sometimes knock hardworking, talented men and women off track. Extending mercy helps them to get back on their feet to hopefully become successful and fulfill their commitments.

Mercy to Employees

As an employer, I also look for opportunities to be merciful to those who work for me. One architect had several emotional breakdowns and was homeless at times. In his younger professional career, he was an outstanding architect with a fine family. But he lost everything due to his illness and homelessness. He came to our office numerous times over several years requesting an interview. Knowing of his issues, every firm had rejected him. But one morning at church when I saw John, I heard God whisper inside my head, "Raymond, I've sent him to you numerous times. When are you going to hire him?"

On Monday morning, I called him, and he was in our office by noon, dressed and ready to work. He worked for our firm for five years before we finally retired him because of his condition. A couple years later, he passed away due to Alzheimer's. Hiring him was a merciful act, but we were the beneficiaries of it. He blessed our firm in more ways than we could ever repay him. There were tough times—it was messy, it caused problems, and it was costly due to some of his mistakes. But nevertheless, we knew that we were to extend mercy to him, and we benefited through him working for us.

I endeavor to understand and love my employees in such a way that I can show them mercy when necessary. We have hired numerous employees who missed the mark in the position for which they were hired, but we have chosen to extend mercy to these low-performing employees. Rather than terminating them, we try moving them to another position. Depending on their personality and temperament, we may confront them in full disclosure or subtly move them. Several employees flourished in their new positions; some employees never found a good fit after two or three moves, so we terminated them. These second chances extended mercy to them because we did not immediately place the hardship of unemployment on them.

Another employee performed his job poorly, so we moved

him around in hopes of finding a better fit. He was cheerful, pleasant, and hardworking, but he was careless and constantly made mistakes. Many years later, he left our employment after receiving numerous second chances.

Forgiveness of Employees and Clients

At times I have struggled to forgive employees who left under bad circumstances. Some employees walked off the job without notice. One secretary went to lunch, leaving her computer on, never to return. Some employees left us in a lurch by giving us one or two days' notice. These examples might lead some to believe we are bad employers, but I do not believe that to be the case. Each individual left for a different reason, usually one that was quite odd by my way of thinking. I had to learn to forgive them because their leaving always put me in a bind. But I found that putting myself in their position, looking from their point of view, made forgiving much easier.

I have had to learn to forgive some of our clients who have verbally abused us in conversations regarding certain projects. We have worked for numerous national corporations, occasionally with less-than-kind clients. Some will call and be demanding; others will yell at us and accuse us of incompetency. They know there will be no consequences to their actions because we are not in a good position to talk back to "the client." This has been difficult for some of our staff—and for me personally. I have learned to forgive them, because I realized that they are under a lot of pressure and have deadlines too. Because I have learned to love my clients, I can let it roll off my back and forgive them when they act this way.

Forgiveness and mercy are integral parts of a successful

business. I have noticed that unforgiving and unmerciful individuals can become stiff-necked, hard to deal with, and prideful. We cannot afford to be that way, because that is not the kind of personality most clients want to deal with. Nor do employees like this attitude in employers.

Striving to be merciful and forgiving makes a business successful as it gives employees and clients security and confidence.

For Further Study

- Matthew 5:7: The merciful shall receive mercy.
- Matthew 6:12; Luke 11:4: The Lord's Prayer—be a conduit of forgiveness.
- Mark 11:12–14, 20–25: Story of the withered fig tree.
- Mark 11:25: When praying, forgive others so that the Father may forgive you.
- Luke 6:36: Be merciful, just as the Father is merciful.
- Luke 6:37: Forgive and you will be forgiven.

23

RECONCILIATION AND PEACEFULNESS

SETTLE WITH ACCUSERS

As large crowds sat on the mountainside, Jesus taught what later became known as the Sermon on the Mount. During his teaching, he said to "settle matters quickly with your adversary who is taking you to court. Do it while you are still together on the way, or your adversary may hand you over to the judge, and the judge may hand you over to the officer, and you may be thrown into prison" (Matthew 5:25 NIV).

Nothing gets our heart pumping faster than a lawsuit or an adversary. The antagonism and threat trigger a strong emotional response, sending us into fight-or-flight mode. I do not like having adversaries. I think Jesus encouraged quick settlements for a good reason—nothing affects our emotional state or causes more distress than being pursued in court. Regardless of whether we are innocent, a heavy burden presses down on us.

I have experienced that feeling numerous times in my business career. I have also had the disappointment of being manipulated, violated, and wronged. I might be justified in pursuing them for remedy, but even if I am in the right, the principle still applies: settle quickly and avoid court.

Countless professionals in our society make a living by going to court; they are known as lawyers. But the best lawyers I have retained hold the perspective that it is better to settle, if possible, than to go to court. This is wise counsel because we are not guaranteed a favorable outcome in a jury trial or by a judge. We are truly at the mercy of the court.

No principle has stuck in my mind more than that of reconciling and settling with my accusers. Through the years, I have been wronged by clients who have not paid an invoice or for work that was done. I had a choice to sue them for payment, but I elected not to because of this principle. Does it mean I should always avoid court? Not necessarily, but I think the principle is to avoid it if possible for our own well-being.

When we were sued over a roof collapse ten years ago, a feeling of heaviness weighed on me for over a year prior to the mediation hearing. We took this principle to heart and entered the mediation with the hope of settling. We were able to settle even though it was a terrifying lawsuit with potentially devastating damages. In the end, the settlement worked out best for all parties.

We have also had frivolous lawsuits filed against our firm. People are notorious for feeling that someone should pay for their mishaps. We have been brought into suits because a lady ran over a man in a parking lot; a man simply fell off a ramp; a person yanked on a grab bar, broke it off the wall, and claimed to be injured; and a store workman tripped and fell while getting out of his truck. These plaintiffs falsely accused our firm of misdeeds. In all the cases, prior to a court date, we exonerated ourselves and had the cases dismissed. In essence, we were settling before we went to court. We have experienced positive outcomes when defending ourselves with the attitude that we avoid the courthouse as much as possible. I am hopeful we can continue to have the right attitude and willingness to humbly settle with our accusers.

When Jesus taught about settling quickly, he was also talking about reconciling with others. He said that if we have something against someone, we need to reconcile prior to coming before God with our requests. The Lord was encouraging us to keep short accounts with people. If we do not, resentment builds, and we eventually harbor bitterness toward that person. That resentment and bitterness will affect our attitude and bleed over into our actions. It is difficult to eradicate bitterness once it sinks its roots into our hearts. I have noticed how easy it is to become embittered toward a client or a consultant because of wrongdoing, but quickly forgiving and reconciling preserves the relationship and fosters future teamwork. Reconciling with others as Jesus suggested is also important for our emotional health and well-being.

The Gospel of Mark encourages us to be at peace with each other: "Salt is good, but if the salt has lost its saltiness, how will you make it salty again? Have salt in yourselves, and be at peace with one another" (Mark 9:50). This does not mean that we cannot have disagreements, but it does mean that we should not be combative or arrogant toward those with whom we disagree. We can disagree with people and yet still be at peace with them.

Business leaders need this skill to work effectively with the broad range of personalities in the workforce.

One way I avoid bitterness and resentment is by endeavoring to love my enemies and to pray for them. I have developed a discipline of praying for those with whom I have issues. Prayer softens my heart and changes my attitude. I have also had a long-term habit of praying for my employees, helping me love them unconditionally, avoid conflicts, and be at peace with them.

When I enter contractual agreements with investment opportunities, I do so with the commitment that I will not sue if there is a breach of contract. My attitude is that we will always work it out. We will settle or renegotiate. But entering a contractual agreement with the idea that you may eventually sue allows bitterness and resentment to subtly creep in.

I have had numerous opportunities to help startup companies with investment capital or private equity loans. Although many have been successful, a few have struggled or failed. If I were prideful, I could be quick to pursue them in court. But I know this is not emotionally good for me, nor is it extending mercy and peace to those I originally entrusted with the funds. Instead, I have chosen to be patient, believing that we will work it out in lieu of going to the courthouse.

Rest assured, I am not a pushover; I am serious with each contractual agreement, but I allow room for negotiations and renegotiations to aid the other party when appropriate. I certainly do not advocate throwing good money after bad, but if the other partners are sincerely working hard with the reasonable hope of making a profit, then extending mercy and having patience are worthwhile. I have been greatly blessed by those who eventually became successful, and I have been rewarded even by those who failed, knowing that my help was well intended, patient, and peaceful.

For Further Study

- ◆ Matthew 5:9: Be a peacemaker in disputes.
- ◆ Matthew 5:23–26; Luke 12:58: Settle quickly with accusers before court.
- ◆ Matthew 5:44–46: Love adversaries. Pray for those who persecute you.
- ◆ Matthew 18:15–17: Confront privately.
- ◆ Mark 9:50: Be at peace with each other.

24

DILIGENCE AND HARD WORK

WE ARE CREATED FOR WORK

There is nothing more holy than diligent hard work. Human-kind was created to work. God's first instructions to Adam were to take care of the garden, to manage and cultivate it to grow. Everything in God's kingdom seems designed to grow. We are to work hard to cultivate growth in God's kingdom through applying his principles.

While writing a book on the business principles found in the Old Testament book of Proverbs, I noticed that the commanding principle for success was to be diligent and work hard. This principle is embedded in the Gospels and is evident in the life of Christ.

Diligence has not been easy for me; it requires me to work whether I feel like it or not. Even in writing this book, I have struggled to complete the task. For me, writing is much like running, and neither comes naturally. But I have developed my writing skills—as I did my running skills—by committing to follow through, to run whether in the inclement cold or scorching heat.

Jesus Set the Example of Diligence

Jesus was excellent in all he did. Throughout his earthly ministry, he worked extremely hard serving all those around him. Jesus had compassion on the crowds, even when he was exhausted or grieving. After the beheading of his cousin and friend, John the Baptist, Jesus withdrew to a desolate place, but when he saw the crowds that followed, he had compassion on them and healed their sick. Jesus worked even while grieving loss as he demonstrated diligence to complete the works of his Father.

Jesus told us that "the gate is narrow and the way is hard that leads to life, and those who find it are few" (Matthew 7:14). While I believe this means that salvation comes only through belief in Christ, there is also a broader application here. Living a righteous life will be difficult because the path is narrow and hard to find in our fallen world system. We must be diligent and work hard to pursue a righteous life.

Prior to launching his public ministry—selecting the first disciples or going to the wedding in Cana—Jesus prepared. He spent the first thirty unrecorded years of his life growing, being educated, working in business, and gaining experience and wisdom.

I have worked hard as an architect in the design business for over thirty-five years. Much of that time, I kept looking in the rearview mirror to see if I had missed something along the way. What I realized was that those years were preparing me for the purpose to which God had always called me. But it took years of diligent hard work to realize my calling as a steward in God's kingdom. The years and preparation were necessary to gain effectiveness.

Jesus put in long hours to accomplish his mission. He tirelessly met with all those he encountered, healing even when he was fatigued. Wherever he went, a multitude surrounded him, seeking to have their needs met. He chose to be diligent in his endless work of bringing the kingdom of God to this earth. Jesus rose early to pray and at times sought solitude to meditate and abide with the Father. Both his hard work and fellowship with the Father are great examples for us to follow.

Pulling All-Nighters

The architectural profession is known for "pulling all-nighters." Students learn early in architectural school what it means to stay up all night working on projects. We are told in numerous accounts that Jesus pulled all-nighters in prayer, which is another example of the diligence and hard work that reflect his character.

Although we have no way of knowing how many people waited in lines or crowded around Jesus for healing, it is safe to assume that the numbers grew as the news of his power spread. The whole time he traveled from village to village in Galilee, many were brought to him to be healed. In several accounts, it was noted that he healed "all those brought to him." Can you imagine the hard work and emotional energy required to heal that many people? Now that is demanding work!

In the Sermon on the Mount, Jesus said, "Let your light shine before others, so that they may see your good works and give glory to your Father who is in heaven" (Matthew 5:16). This assumes that you are working and that the things you are doing are worthwhile, wholesome, and good for others to observe. Jesus let his light shine before others through his good works, thus glorifying his Father in heaven.

God appeals to our human nature by offering us rewards for our hard work. Most of the stewardship parables have a reward awaiting those who are faithful. These are designed by God to stimulate and encourage us to work hard.

I run half marathons as a hobby. Reaching the finish line and receiving a medal around my neck is a great reward for my diligent effort in preparing for the race. It may seem hokey, but I enjoy receiving the bling even though it is an inexpensive piece of metal that may not mean much in future years. The point is that it is a reward. Imagine how much greater our motivation should be to diligently pursue the works God has prepared for us, knowing that our heavenly reward exceeds what we can ever imagine.

Parables about Agriculture

The parables are mostly agricultural in nature. Everything from working in the vineyard, to sowing seeds, to the laborers in the field emphasizes the necessity of hard work. Work is required for results, and results are required for success. Even the parable about the treasure hidden in the field involved work to find the treasure. Most of these parables have the embedded idea that work is required to receive a reward. In contrast, the lazy steward in the parable of the talents did nothing with the master's money but hide it. He was condemned for his laziness and not putting that money to work.

The Parable of Two Sons

Another parable illustrated the difference between two sons who were asked by their father to do something. One son gave lip service, agreeing to the request but then failed to follow through. The second son told the father that he would not do it, but later did what his father asked.

The one who does something is more valuable to a business owner than the one who gives lip service. It is better to find employees who do what you ask of them, because "doers" always prove to be more valuable for results in business than "talkers."

The Apostles

It is interesting to note the kind of men Jesus selected as his apostles. The first was Andrew, who brought his brother, Peter. As you study the life of Peter in historical accounts, you find that he probably had the largest fishing conglomerate in the town of Capernaum. Tradition credits Peter with the largest home in his town, indicating his success. He may have owned one of the largest businesses on the Sea of Galilee. He had at least two partners in business, including James and John, who also became Jesus' apostles. They all worked hard, as can be seen in the account of their fishing all-nighter. John was well known and granted entrance into the high priest's house during Jesus' trial. This may have been due to his fishing business, as tradition associates John with the fish concession in Jerusalem. Clearly, Jesus selected several of his apostles from among hard-working fishermen.

Excellence and Diligence

Through my experience as a professional, I have found that excellence and diligence are sisters. I cannot be an excellent architect without being a diligent worker. Excellence does not result from talent alone; it is developed through hard work. Few would hire a sloppy, lazy architect, no matter how talented, but they will hire a diligent hard worker, even if he or she makes occasional mistakes. I feel the same with my employees. If they are working hard, we can easily get through the mistakes. But it is frustrating to deal with a lazy employee who makes mistakes.

For Further Study

- ◆ Genesis 2:15: God's instructions to Adam.
- ◆ Matthew 14:13–14: Jesus healed even while grieving loss.
- ◆ Matthew 21:28–32: Parable of two sons.

25

EXCELLENCE

WALKING ON WATER

A s in any honorable profession, excellence is a requirement to thrive in business. Nobody in his or her right mind would go back to an incompetent physician, a careless accountant, or an unscrupulous attorney. Similarly, no one returns to an architect who provides sloppy drawings or misses details resulting in construction cost overruns. Our firm's culture is built around excellence. Without it, we have nothing to offer.

We drive excellence down to the finest of details. I like to use the phrase, "type the right email address," because even a small mistake such as a period or an underscore ensures one thing: the email will not be delivered. The Lord does not require perfection, nor does society expect professionals or businesspeople to be perfect in all they do, but competence and a standard of excellence are required in anything considered a profession.

Jesus did everything with excellence. Whether because of

a conscious demonstration of quality or just his natural inclination, Jesus was the perfect manifestation of excellence in everything he did and said. Mark 7:37 says people were amazed at how Jesus did everything well. He didn't just try to heal people, nor did he treat them haphazardly. Whether he was fatigued or under pressure, the deaf began to hear, the mute began to speak, and the demons fled. His miracles were done with excellence; the infirmities did not reappear. In fact, when John the Baptist sent his disciples to ask Jesus if he was the Messiah, he replied, "Go and tell John what you hear and see: the blind receive their sight and the lame walk, lepers are cleansed and the deaf hear, and the dead are raised up, and the poor have good news preached to them" (Matthew 11:4–5).

My favorite instance of Jesus performing excellent work is his converting water to wine while attending a wedding in Cana of Galilee. John's Gospel notes this as the first manifestation of his miracles. He performed it in a natural setting; there was no fanfare or great acclamation for what he had done. His mother knew that he was the Savior, having been told prior to his birth by an angel and having witnessed his early years. So when she saw that the wine had run out, she told the servants at the wedding to do whatever Jesus instructed. He told them to fill the wash jars to the brim with water. The jars are estimated to have held twenty to thirty gallons each, making 120 to 180 gallons of wine total. Without explanation or tasting, he said, "Now draw some out and take it to the master of the feast" (John 2:8).

The master of the feast then exclaimed to the bridegroom, "Everyone serves the good wine first, and when the people have drunk freely, then the poor wine. But you have kept the good wine until now" (John 2:10). Jesus demonstrated that when he performed a miracle, he did not just meet minimal standards but surpassed them with undeniable excellence.

At times, the multitudes followed Jesus into areas that did not have villages or places to obtain food. Being compassionate, Jesus did not want to send them away hungry lest they faint on their journey home. So he fed them. The two well-known feedings involved four thousand and five thousand men. Since these numbers did not include the women and children, Jesus actually fed as many as ten thousand to fifteen thousand on each of these occasions. Jesus performed these miracles with such excellence that all were satisfied with leftovers to spare.

Jesus delegated the responsibility of feeding these people to his disciples. He told them to have the multitudes sit down on the green grass in groups of fifties and hundreds and then to distribute the food he had blessed. In one case, it was five loaves and two fish; in another, it was seven loaves and a few fish. Jesus organized and efficiently fed these great multitudes by utilizing his disciples in performing the miracle. By itself, this was excellent leadership; he didn't just show them what he could do, but he involved them in key roles. We can't begin to understand the physics of this multiplication of food, but we know that multitudes were fed and satisfied and that the gathered scraps far exceeded the initial supply.

I love how the miracles are irrefutable because of the evidence. The conversion of water to wine happened in huge water jars used for purification; the feeding of the multitudes grew out of a child's lunch of a few loaves and fish. Yet the unknowing steward of the banquet commended the wine, and the disciples picked up basketfuls of scraps. Reading these accounts should dispel all doubt that these miracles occurred.

When I was growing up, I heard my mother say, "That person could walk on water," meaning that a person was perfect, above reproach, and excellent in everything he or she did. Of course, she was referring to Jesus walking on water. That was one of the greatest of Jesus' miracles, demonstrating his authority over nature as Creator.

When Jesus walked across the Sea of Galilee to meet his disciples on the other side, he did so without flourish and in the middle of the night. We know the story well—he called Peter out to him and gave Peter the power to walk on water. I suspect he did all of this to prove to those most dear to him that he truly was God.

In another of his miracles, he was asleep in the back of the boat as the disciples crossed the Sea of Galilee. When a furious storm engulfed them, nearly swamping the boat with waves, the panicked disciples awoke Jesus. He stood up, rebuked the wind and the waves, and immediately calmed the sea, proving that his power was irrefutable and excellent. What Jesus did in his miracles is the epitome of excellence, demonstrating his power to overcome nature. We do not have the ability to overcome nature, but we do have the ability to follow his example in excellence.

Jesus did everything well, even to the end. While hanging on the cross, he saw his mother and John, the disciple whom he loved. Amid his agony, he acknowledged his mother and assigned her care to someone he could trust. Jesus took care of everyone perfectly, even when he was in distress, suffering, and being tortured. His excellence was exemplified in his ultimate sacrifice.

When You Want It Done Right

Because of our determination to provide quality professional service, we developed a reputation with our major clients for doing just that. Seeking honest feedback, I once asked Walmart's vice president of construction, "What is your opinion of our firm?" He replied that when you want it done right, you use RHA Architects—otherwise, any other firm would do. His words reassured us that we were meeting our goal of excellence.

But excellence is a high ideal that can be executed only when we pay attention to the details. Excellence in the important things begins with the seemingly insignificant. To be excellent, we must do everything with effort and concentration. We cannot be sloppy and indifferent; we must be focused and intense. Excellence is not an accident but a determined effort that sometimes pushes us beyond what we think we can accomplish.

For me, professionally, excellence did not happen immediately. I always pushed myself, staying up late, getting up early, working extremely hard to develop an attitude of excellence. I have found that diligence and hard work are the shortest routes to excellence. But most are not willing to put in the effort because work is hard and diligence is taxing.

We have little to offer without excellence. People who make excuses for lacking excellence frustrate me. "I didn't have enough time." "I wasn't paid enough money." "It really doesn't matter, because in God's kingdom that thing is not important." Excellence depends on your effort, not external circumstances, and God considers everything in his kingdom important. Jesus *did* sweat the details; his excellence in all things expresses love and testifies to the nature of God's kingdom.

Anytime we work with others, we appreciate the excellence they bring to the team. Excellence is a prerequisite for having a profound impact on people as a Christian, and I have told myself many times, *Don't tell people you're good; just show it to them.* Nothing speaks louder than quality work, and, in my opinion, nothing is more holy in God's kingdom than excellent work.

When I go to an auto mechanic, I appreciate a job well done. I choose a mechanic based on his excellence, not his faith, because I want my car fixed properly. If he is a Christian, then that is a bonus and an extra blessing, but I don't appreciate him telling me about his faith if he cannot fix my car. The same is true when we are in dire need of medical care. My main concern is not that my cardiologist is a Christian; I just want an excellent one. I certainly do not condone using immoral, unscrupulous, or evil professionals, but excellence is my first requirement when selecting others with whom to work.

Work in God's kingdom deserves our best effort to achieve excellence. I have witnessed just the opposite among many Christians who feel like grace will cover their ineptness or lack of effort. When God created the earth, he declared his works to be good, perfect in excellence, and lacking nothing. God does not demand perfection from us, but he does rejoice in our pursuit of excellence as those created in his image.

For Further Study

- Matthew 12:15; 15:29–31; Luke 4:40; 6:19: Jesus healed them all.

- Matthew 14:13–21; Mark 6:30–44; Luke 9:10–17: The feeding of the five thousand.
- Matthew 14:20; 15:37; Mark 6:42; 8:8; Luke 9:17: They were all satisfied.
- Matthew 14:22–33: Jesus walked on water and calmed the storm.
- Matthew 15:32–39; Mark 8:1–9: The feeding of the four thousand.
- Mark 4:35–41: Jesus calmed the sea.
- Mark 7:37: Jesus did everything well.
- John 2:1–11: The changing of water to wine.
- John 9:1–39: Jesus healed a blind man.
- John 19:25–27: Jesus cared for his mother at the cross.

26

STEWARDSHIP

THE WIDOW'S COINS

Stewardship is about managing the assets of someone else. In running our firm, we have learned the true meaning of stewardship. Our stewardship responsibilities range from how we charge for our time and expenses to how we bill our clients. It includes maintaining low overhead and allocating our staff to be most efficient. We recognize it is our client's money that is used to pay for our services. It is our responsibility to take diligent care of our clients and their resources as stewards entrusted with their projects.

Reflecting on stewardship, Jesus said, "One who is faithful in a very little is also faithful in much, and one who is dishonest in a very little is also dishonest in much" (Luke 16:10). This dialogue was about money and our hearts, and he went on to say, "If you have not been faithful in that which is another's, who will give you that which is your own?" (Luke 16:12).

We have endeavored to be good stewards for our clients. For over thirty years, they have entrusted us with thousands of projects to design, permit, and ensure that the construction meets the quality standards of our professional documents. We are privileged to be entrusted with so much by the world's largest architectural client. Along with this privilege comes tremendous accountability. Luke 12:48 says, "Everyone to whom much was given, of him much will be required, and from him to whom they entrusted much, they will demand the more."

Our clients hold us accountable for their projects. Their trust grows out of this accountability and is best fostered if we are found faithful when no one is looking or when we are least suspecting. When our clients find us faithful, their natural reaction is to reward us with more work. This aligns with the principle in Luke 19:26, "To everyone who has, more will be given."

This principle was derived from the parable of the ten minas that I mentioned briefly in chapter nine. In the parable, a man of noble birth gave ten of his servants a mina apiece. At that time, a mina was valued at approximately three months of a laborer's wage. He charged them, "Put this money to work until I come back." Upon his return, he called the servants to account. The first servant said, "Sir, your mina has earned ten more." The master replied, "Well done, my good servant! Because you have been trustworthy in a very small matter, take charge of ten cities." This was a large reward for proving faithful in his stewardship. The second servant retuned five minas and was rewarded with taking charge of five cities.

Another servant came and said, "Sir, here is your mina; I have kept it laid away in a piece of cloth. I was afraid of you, because you are a hard man. You take out what you did not put in and reap what you did not sow." The master judged him by his own words, calling him a wicked servant, and asked, "Why then didn't you put my money on deposit, so that when I came back, I could have collected it with interest?" Then an interesting thing happened. The master ordered those standing by, "Take his mina away from him and give it to the one who has ten minas." When the servants were astounded by this command, the master replied, "I tell you that to everyone who has, more will be given, but as for the one who has nothing, even what they have will be taken away."

In working with our employees, I have noticed that the faithful ones are those who work hard and use their time well. They are usually rewarded with more to manage. Because they take proper care with the little things, we can entrust them with more important tasks. Those who are faithful and hardworking are those who excel. Eventually, many of them move into management and some into the ownership of our firm.

Similar to the parable of the ten minas is the parable that Jesus taught about the talents. A master entrusted his servants with his wealth. Talents were given to each of the servants according to their abilities. The servant who was given five talents immediately put the money to work and doubled it. Although not instructed to do so, he did it on his own initiative, demonstrating his motivation to work hard for his master. The servant who was given two talents did the same. But the servant who was given one talent buried it because he was lazy and lived in fear.

A talent might have been worth twenty years of wages. Some estimate it was equivalent to seventy-five pounds, possibly of gold, which is a phenomenal amount. We are unsure of the exact value of a talent, but we get the picture. When the master called his servants to account for what they had done, the one who had five talents returned with five more. The master responded, "Well done, good and faithful servant." The servant who had been given two talents also doubled his investment. Both servants greatly increased what had been entrusted to them.

The point of the parable was to show their faithfulness in honoring their master with the talents. Both good stewards received equivalent rewards and commendation from the master. The servant who buried his talent in the ground was shamed, being called wicked and lazy.

Stewardship of Increase

In business, we must increase what our clients or customers have entrusted to us. This may mean giving more service than was paid for, but the reward will be returning customers and future business. The stewardship of our time is important, particularly for professional service firms that bill for their time. Being a good steward means utilizing our time wisely during the day so that we give the client the best value. It is important that when we are examined carefully, we are found to be above reproach. A good steward of his or her time is faithful even when no one is looking and is found to be faithful when he or she least expects to be assessed. This steward is a great blessing to not only the employer but also the client.

Everyone wants a return on his or her investment. That is what the masters in the parables were looking for when they called their servants to give an account for what had been entrusted to them. Stewardship aims to faithfully transact the business of increase, because the master always expects a return on his or her investment.

It is my opinion as a business leader that we should not entrust important things to individuals who cannot take care of them. We ensure that certain employees are not entrusted with critical projects or client meetings if they have not proved trustworthy. We only reward stewardship to those who have demonstrated faithfulness in the smallest of details. Minute details, if ignored, could result in catastrophic mistakes. Entrusting stewardship only to the faithful complies with the exhortation of Matthew 7:6: "Do not give dogs what is holy, and do not throw your pearls before the pigs, lest they trample them underfoot and turn to attack you."

In the kingdom of God, everything grows. Everything grows around the trustworthy steward as well. Anyone who entrusts an asset to a steward wants to see growth. Many of Jesus' stewardship parables utilized farming and the agrarian economy, ranging from the planting of seeds that grew into a great harvest to the harvesting of good fruit from good trees. An example is the mustard seed that began as the smallest of seeds but grew into the largest of plants; in fact, it grew so large that even birds would nest in it. This exhibits the phenomenal growth that occurs within God's kingdom.

Multiplication is an indicator of good stewardship, as illustrated in the parable of the different soils. The seeds in good soil yielded a crop thirty, sixty, or a hundred times what was planted. As faithful stewards, we plant the seeds, but God causes the growth. Seeds in good soil produce fantastic crops, just as phenomenal growth can occur when God blesses the stewardship of faithful men and women.

Stewardship of Our Clients

Over the years, I have been astonished by how the Lord has blessed our firm and allowed it to increase in size. We started with a few small projects and, at last count, we had completed over eight thousand projects in the past thirty years. The proliferation of this work is hard to fathom in our profession. When I meet people for the first time, I ask them where they grew up— chances are we have done a project in their hometown. With few exceptions, everyone I have ever talked to has been inside a project that our firm produced.

We endeavor to be good stewards of our clients by developing services for what they actually need. We do not oversell but seek to be prudent in what we provide for them. If we provide our clients with excellent value, then we have stewarded our relationship well and they recognize the worth in continuing with us. Stewarding a client well is critical to staying in business.

Stewardship within Our Firm

We take care with not only our client's assets but our own as well. Many consider their important assets to be equipment, software, and office environment. We regard our people as our most important assets. We seek to employ our people in the most efficient and effective way. We try to give them a great environment to work in and a challenging job that enables them to feel they are accomplishing their own goals. We endeavor to pay them well, but we also utilize their talents to the greatest extent possible so that they feel fulfilled and therefore provide the best possible service to our clients.

We keep our office environment clean, organized, and efficient. Stewarding our environment well helps us remain profitable because we do not waste time and effort on clutter and disorganization. We buy top-of-the-line equipment and take good care of it so we can use it for years.

Our firm has remained in the same physical location for over twenty-five years through shrewd negotiations that lowered our overhead. Our office space is creative and stimulating for our artistic profession. It is simple and open, accentuating the historic setting of an old warehouse building. By remaining in the same office, we have saved on moving and new construction finish-out costs.

Just as in the parable of the seed that grows, the story of our firm is one of growth. Our income has far exceeded expectations. This is due in part to being good stewards, but even more, it is due to the kind blessings of God.

Honor God with Our Wealth

Another principle of stewardship is to give back the firstfruits to God. I look at our growth as an opportunity to be a blessing to God by investing in his kingdom. Several parables and stories show us examples of honoring God with our money and assets.

The poor widow exemplified this by honoring God with the two small coins she placed in the temple treasury. She gave all she had to live on. This was her way of glorifying and worshiping God. She has been immortalized for her stewardship, and, in my opinion, she is the best steward of the Bible.

While Jesus was eating dinner at a Pharisee's house, a woman who had lived a sinful life anointed him with an alabaster jar of expensive perfume (Luke 7:36–38). Later, Mary anointed Jesus with a pint of pure nard, also expensive perfume, by pouring it on his feet and wiping his feet with her hair (John 12:1–5). The disciples were indignant because of the costliness of this perfume and, in their opinion, the waste of it all. In fact, the perfume is said to have cost a year's wage. In today's terms, for the average worker, this might mean as much as twenty thousand dollars. I cannot imagine spending that much money on someone. These women spent a phenomenal amount of money, challenging us with their extravagant generosity in honoring Jesus.

In contrast, Jesus told a parable about a vineyard and its tenants. After carefully preparing the vineyard, the landowner rented it to some tenants with the expectation that they would provide him with fruit from the harvest. The tenants of the vineyard did not honor their landowner with fruit from the harvest. In fact, when the landowner sent his servant to collect the fruit, they beat him. The landowner then sent several more servants to collect; they were also beaten. Finally, he sent his son, whom they killed. The tenants refused to give the landowner his portion of the profits and killed his son in their plot to take his inheritance for themselves. When the landowner came to the vineyard, he brought the wicked tenants to a wretched end and gave the vineyard to other tenants who would give him his share of the crop at harvest time.

Although Jesus told this parable regarding the chief priests and Pharisees, the principles of the story apply to us, because God has entrusted each of us with a vineyard to steward. In my case, it has been my profession and business. To be true stewards, we must recognize that God has given us our businesses, and we should honor him with the firstfruits of our vineyards.

We honor God with our wealth when we use our resources to accomplish what is most important to his heart. Matthew 25:31–46 makes it clear that someday we will stand before him to give an account of what has been entrusted to us. Jesus said that we will account for how we take care of those who cannot take care of themselves. We are to use our resources to take care of his kingdom. Taking care of his kingdom includes defending the weak, feeding the hungry, protecting the vulnerable, and providing for those with needs. If we want to guarantee that treasures await us in heaven, then we must utilize our wealth to take care of the poor. Then when we stand before the judgment seat, our Master will tell us, "Well done, my good and faithful servant."

Stewardship of Profit

An important part of our firm's stewardship is setting aside profit. We use this allotted profit to take good care of our employees, to give them bonuses, and to maintain a margin for tough times ahead. If we consumed everything we made, we would lose this margin, be at the mercy of the times, and be forced to make desperate decisions.

We strive to be good stewards of our clients and how we handle our overhead. We keep our overhead low, we do not waste office supplies, and we do not waste people's time. I have tried to drive this principle home with my employees. We are the stewards of our business. We are also stewards of the profit made in our business through our hardworking employees. The profit is not for our own consumption; we are to use it to take care of our employees while stewarding the remainder in a manner that glorifies God.

For Further Study

- Matthew 7:6: Entrust to the faithful, and do not throw your assets away.
- Matthew 13:1–43: Parables about growth.
- Matthew 13:12; Luke 8:18: To the one who has, more will be given.
- Matthew 13:23, 31–33: The evidence of good stewardship is multiplication.
- Matthew 21:33–41; Luke 20:9–18: Parable of the wicked tenants.
- Matthew 21:43: The kingdom is given to those producing fruit.
- Matthew 24:45–47; Luke 12:42–44: The faithful steward.
- Matthew 25:14–30: Parable of the talents.
- Matthew 25:21: The essence of stewardship.
- Matthew 25:28–29: Good stewards will be given more to steward.
- Matthew 26:6–13; Mark 14:3–9: Woman anointed Jesus.
- Mark 12:41–44; Luke 21:1–4: The poor widow at the temple.
- Luke 12:48: To whom much is given, much is expected.
- Luke 16:12: Taking care of someone else's assets.
- Luke 19:11–27: Parable of the ten minas.
- Luke 20:9–18: Parable of the wicked tenants.
- John 15:16: Stewards are chosen to bear fruit.

27

THE ULTIMATE DESIGN
OF BUSINESS

recently sat in my office with my feet on the desk while reading a ministry newsletter after a good breakfast. What captured my attention was a quote from Richard Stearns, president of World Vision. Stearns was offering his paraphrase of the parable of the final judgment in Matthew 25:

> For I was hungry, while you had all you needed. I was thirsty, but you drank bottled water. I was a stranger, and you wanted me deported. I needed clothes, but you needed more clothes. I was sick, and you pointed out the behaviors that led to my sickness. I was in prison, and you said I was getting what I deserved.[5]

My heart broke as I asked myself, What is on God's heart? What am I doing about it? Sitting comfortably in my nice office, I contemplated, What is the chief purpose of business in God's kingdom? Could it be important for my business to develop and maintain an economic engine to take care of others?

Building the Engine

A goal of any business is to generate profits. If it doesn't, it can't sustain itself and will subsequently die. So the default setting and nature of healthy business is to generate profits. I view our architectural firm much like an economic engine to generate profits. It has taken us a long time to build an effective economic engine that is sustainable and runs efficiently.

Any mechanical engine must be fueled and maintained. The oil, filters, and belts must be changed. The engine must be lubricated. No matter how well you take care of the engine, some parts will break, wear out, and need to be replaced. This is where improvement and innovation come in, such as the hiring of talented people and the upgrading of equipment. Eventually the engine may wear out, but over its lifetime it will have served a useful purpose in the grand scheme. Just as with a mechanical engine, if the economic engine is maintained by the owners of the business, it provides beneficial economic results for a long time.

In the first chapter of this book, I thanked God for not letting fear talk me into a U-turn. As glad as I was to walk away from that initial meeting with Walmart over thirty years ago with nineteen projects committed to my fledgling firm, I *never* could have foreseen the economic engine that would result. Eight thousand projects and a half-billion dollars in revenue have sustained the families of more than 350 professionals over that time span. Adding the contributions the firm has made to ministries and other charitable organizations just magnifies the purpose of business in God's kingdom.

Transferring Treasures to Heaven

As Jesus explained to the disciples, a time will come when everyone will be gathered and he will separate all humankind into two groups. One group will inherit the kingdom of God, and the other group will be condemned (Matthew 25:31–34). If this is the final accounting, then what it reveals should drive our business goals. The group that God blessed with an inheritance were those who faithfully met the needs of "the least." Jesus mentioned multiple ways to do this; I interpret them to mean:

- Feed the hungry: meet basic needs.
- Satisfy the thirsty: spread the gospel.
- Welcome strangers: assist immigrants, foreigners, and those of other cultures.
- Clothe the naked: provide work with sustainable businesses.
- Heal and visit the sick: provide medical and health-care opportunities.
- Visit the prisoners: provide justice.

"You Did It for Me"

Although it is a bold statement, I argue that the ultimate design of business within God's economy is to become an economic engine that funnels profits to help those in need. If we do this as businessmen and businesswomen, "the King will reply, 'Truly I tell you, whatever you did for one of the least of these brothers and sisters of mine, you did for me'" (Matthew 25:40 NIV).

God has designed us to work for rewards. In the parables that relate particularly to stewardship, there is always a reward for the faithful. For me, that is a motivation to succeed.

Final Encouragement

Our business and our employment opportunities give us the wonderful privilege of working in God's kingdom while on earth. As businessmen and businesswomen, we are stewards entrusted with assets. We use our jobs, professions, and businesses as economic engines to take care of those around us, especially those on God's heart. We develop businesses to take care of our families and to offer our employees good jobs. We produce products and provide services to benefit humanity, and we use the profits to glorify God. If we consume all we make and share nothing with those in need, then what makes us different from the farmer who built larger barns?

May the parables from the Gospels in the New Testament challenge us as businesspeople to become stewards in God's kingdom. May we become his hands and feet on earth, taking care of those who cannot take care of themselves. May we be found faithful with righteous hearts that store up treasures in heaven. May everyone look upon us as loving, merciful, and compassionate servants of God our Father and Jesus our King.

It is my hope that our actions will exemplify the fruit of righteousness for his honor and glory.

ACKNOWLEDGMENTS

This book would not have been possible without my faithful assistant, Lisa Vasquez, and the skillful editing of Jenny Buie and Steve Gardner. Many thanks to the BroadStreet team, especially Bill Watkins, Ryan Adair, David Sluka, and Chris Garborg.

I would like to dedicate this book to my children, Stephen Harris and Carrie Arnold, who represent kindness and sweetness in life. I am inadequate without the partnership of Marydel, who lives a precious life of mercy and faithfulness.

NOTES

1   *Merriam-Webster.com*, s.v., "deference," accessed June 15, 2017, https://www.merriam-webster.com/dictionary/deference.

2   *Merriam-Webster.com*, s.v., "service," accessed June 15, 2017, https://www.merriam-webster.com/dictionary/service.

3   *Merriam-Webster.com*, s.v., "humility," accessed June 15, 2017, https://www.merriam-webster.com/dictionary/humility.

4   *Merriam-Webster.com*, s.v., "sacrifice," accessed June 15, 2017, https://www.merriam-webster.com/dictionary/sacrifice.

5   Richard Stearns, *The Hole in Our Gospel* (Nashville: Thomas Nelson, 2009, 2010), 59.

ABOUT THE AUTHOR

 Raymond H. Harris is a practicing archi-
tect, executive movie producer, and venture
capitalist in God's kingdom. He is founder
and chairman of RHA Architects, which has
become one of the largest architectural firms
specializing in corporate architecture.

Raymond graduated first in his class
from the University of Oklahoma and was selected as the outstanding senior in the College of Architecture. He was selected
as the outstanding alumni in 2013–2014.

He cofounded the Christian Economic Forum, is a founding
partner of the Global Cities Movement Day efforts in NYC, and
is extensively involved in international sustainable community
development projects in Africa and Asia. He serves on numerous corporate and not-for-profit boards.

Raymond has authored *The Anatomy of a Successful Firm*
and *The Heart of Business*. He is also an executive producer for
numerous movies distributed by Sony Pictures and Lions Gate
Entertainment. Raymond has hiked all of the continental US
National Parks and served as a Boy Scout scoutmaster.

Raymond and his wife, Marydel, are blessed by their four
adult children, their spouses, and six grandchildren.

ABOUT RAYMOND'S COMPANY

Raymond Harris & Associates Architects (RHA) is one of the most prolific large architectural firms in the United States. Professional services have been provided for projects in almost every municipality in the United States, having worked in all fifty states and in most jurisdictions. It is safe to say that everyone has been in a project that RHA has designed in the past thirty-five years.

RHA has consistently been in the top ten largest firms in the Dallas Metropolitan Area and the state of Texas. At one point, they were one of the top thirty largest firms in the United States. Selected five times as a top five firm in their industry, RHA was selected by McGraw-Hill Publishing as the number two corporate retail design firm for three years.

The firm has provided employment for over 350 employees, most of whom are professionals, and has been a training ground for young architects for decades. By providing excellent service, the firm relies on repeat and referral work.